THE JOURNEY OF A LIFETIME

THE JOURNEY OF A LIFETIME

MARTHA REAPSOME

Harold Shaw Publishers
Wheaton, Illinois

ISBN 0-87788-416-1

Cover design by David LaPlaca

Cover photo © 1993 by Jim Wright

Library of Congress Cataloging-in-Publication Data

Reapsome, Martha, 1932—
    The journey of a lifetime : discovering the joy of walking with
    God / Martha Reapsome.
       p. cm.
    Rev. ed. of: A woman's path to godliness. c1986.
    ISBN 0-87788-416-1
    1. Christian women—Religious life. 2. Reapsome, Martha, 1932-
    I. Reapsome, Martha, 1932 Woman's path to godliness.
  II. Title.
  BV4527.R42 1993
  248.8-43—dc20   92-44923
                                             CIP

---

99   98   97   96   95   94   93

10 9 8 7 6 5 4 3 2 1

To my mother,
who pointed me
to the path to godliness

Contents

Preface

"I'd like you to write a book about godliness," an editor requested over the phone.

"You want to talk to my husband. He's the writer in the family," I said.

"No, I want to talk to you. I want a book on becoming a godly woman. I read an article you wrote on the subject, and I think you're the one to write the book," he insisted.

I retreated and told him I could give him the names of three women who could write the book. "As a matter of fact," I said, "I'll see one of them this weekend. I'll ask her to call you."

He reluctantly agreed.

All day Saturday, at the retreat, I tried to get to JoAnn to give her the editor's message and number. But every time I saw her, someone blocked my way like a Mack truck.

As I described my frustration to my husband the next day, he smiled and said, "Don't you think you'd better pray about it before you say no?"

"I don't want to pray about it because I don't want to do it," I shot back. "Writing is hard work, and I don't want to learn."

But pray about it I did.

A few weeks later we listened to a sermon on Jonah. No, I didn't think I was running away from God like Jonah did. But as the pastor worked his way through the story, the Holy Spirit made two startling connections in my mind. Once Jonah decided to obey God and set out to preach in Nineveh, God was obligated to provide everything Jonah needed to complete his assignment.

Wow! If God assigned me to write this book, then God was on call to provide everything I needed for the assignment. And I could remind him of that fact as often as necessary.

Even more intriguing was the thought that when Jonah started out for Nineveh he had no idea what God planned to do there. God's plans for Nineveh exceeded anything Jonah could imagine.

Could it be that God had a purpose for this book bigger than I could ever dream? Humbled by the thought, I confessed my fears and deep sense of inadequacy. "God, if this assignment is really from you, not from this editor, then I set myself to obey. But you're responsible to provide what I need to do it. I can't imagine what your plans are. But please fulfill your purposes. May you be honored by the book as you were in Nineveh."

Responses to the first edition of *A Women's Path to Godliness* (1986) demonstrated that God's purposes did exceed my small expectations.

"I gave your book to one of my Bible study friends and she said, 'It's like one of my Bibles.'"

"I've read the chapter on trust four times. Have you thought of having the book translated into German? I know many people here in Austria would benefit."

"I teach young married women in Sunday school and would like a copy for each of them. Your book stands ten feet tall. Thank you for writing it."

The instructions in Psalm 145 took on new urgency recently, when I became a grandmother.

> *One generation will commend your works to another; they will tell of your mighty acts. They will speak of the glorious splendor of your majesty, and I will meditate on your wonderful works.*
>
> Psalm 145:4-5

At first reading, I assumed the older generation would be telling the younger generations about God's majesty and power. But I realized the younger generation can teach the older also when I heard about three-year-old Rachel.

"Jesus helped me find you," Rachel announced to her mother, as she ran into the room. "I didn't know where you were and I was afraid. So I asked Jesus to help me find you."

I want our granddaughter, Catherine, to hear the wonderful deeds of God from her parents, grandparents, aunts, uncles, cousins, teachers, pastors, friends.

In this revised edition I've added insights into God's "core curriculum" on godliness from three generations. Women from

25 to 85 commend God's works for our meditation. May their stories encourage you to tell another generation about the great deeds of our God.

Chapter One

Crossroads and Cul-de-Sacs Ahead

Entering the path to godliness

On a cool but sunny Memorial Day afternoon on a lush hillside in Pittsburgh's Schenley Park, to the background noises of the crowd's cheering the Pirates in nearby Forbes Field and the lilting music of a bagpipe player, I became engaged to Jim. That really was a Memorial Day!

After months of eagerly devoured letters and the occasional all-too-short dates when he stopped off at Columbus, Ohio, on his trips between Chicago and Philadelphia, I knew that afternoon, *He's the man.* Just how completely he had swept me off my feet I discovered that night when we went to dinner. For the first time in my life, I had no appetite. I couldn't eat.

For someone who had fought the battle of the bulge all her life, it was an amazing occurrence. I'd heard tales about love stealing one's appetite, but I never believed it actually happened.

But between that day and our wedding the next February, I lost fifteen pounds that I never regained. What a delightful weight-loss program!

How was I so attracted by this seemingly ten-foot-tall man? It all began at the campus of Bowling Green State University in Ohio. InterVarsity Christian Fellowship students had invited Jim Reapsome to come over from the InterVarsity office in Chicago to speak during the annual Religious Emphasis Week. Since I was the InterVarsity staff worker for Ohio, my duties called me to help with dorm discussions. For three evenings Jim dialogued with students about Jesus Christ and how his claims touch our lives. Both his communication skills and his warmth impressed me. Even the collegians who raised the toughest questions appreciated his thoughtful, courteous responses. By the end of the week, I had a new friend.

A couple of months later, shocking news came in a letter from InterVarsity. Jim's wife, Evelyn, had died of a cerebral hemorrhage a few hours after the birth of their son. I cried for my new friend as I pictured him helplessly alone with two-year-old Sara and baby John. "Oh, God, have mercy on him and help him," I wept. "Please meet all his needs and comfort him."

What if you're the one to help meet his needs? flashed through my mind.

"Lord, I'm sorry I thought that. I don't know where that thought came from," I stammered in bewilderment. "But if that thought was from you, you speak to Jim about it." Believe it or not, I completely forgot about that prayer, although I did remember to pray for Jim from time to time. We didn't see each other again until the InterVarsity national staff conference in January at picturesque Bear Trap Ranch, six thousand feet up in the mountains west of Colorado Springs. Crisp, cold air, towering rocks against a brilliant Colorado blue sky, drifts of powdery snow, and the bubbling mountain creek rushing under the footbridge produced a winter wonderland. Jim looked well, considering everything. At one of the worship services, in recounting some of the ways that God had helped him, Jim read:

To comfort all who mourn,
and provide for those who grieve
in Zion—
to bestow on them a crown of beauty
instead of ashes,
the oil of gladness
instead of mourning,
and a garment of praise
instead of a spirit of despair.
They will be called oaks of
righteousness,
a planting of the LORD
for the display of his splendor.

Isaiah 61:2-3

He emphasized beauty for ashes, gladness for mourning, and praise for despair. And I saw an oak of righteousness. He was a man planted and tended by God for a display of God's splendor.

Each evening after the meetings, we all crowded into the dining hall to chat around a tray of fresh fruit. I didn't realize what was going on, but every time I stood by the trash barrel to peel an orange, Jim peeled one on the other side of the barrel. Somehow, we still had lots to talk about when everyone else had finished.

In February, InterVarsity sent a team that included me to shoot a film at the University of Michigan, Ann Arbor. Since Jim was public relations director, he not only supervised the project but also found time to chauffeur the women staff. Oblivious to his strategy, I just thought it was a nice touch—that's all.

At the same time, my father was in a Louisville hospital anxiously awaiting surgery. As the doctor's reports grew increasingly dismal, Mother asked me to come home to be with her and Daddy. She was not well. I knew that she couldn't endure alone those long hours of sitting in the hospital.

Jim kindly offered to take me to the airport, which was an hour's drive away. For some reason, he told me that he was leaving InterVarsity to take a new position in Philadelphia. He also asked, "Do you have a driver's license?"

"No, I don't," I said, curious about such a strange question. "We haven't had a car since Daddy had a heart attack. That was before I was old enough to learn to drive."

"Every woman should have a driver's license," he said sagely. "She never knows when she'll need it."

Chalk it up to small talk, I thought. Like the eyes of those Syrian soldiers chasing the prophet Elisha, my eyes were blinded, figuratively speaking. Back on campus, someone who did see what was going on was Jim's good friend, Paul

Little. After the airport trip, he teased Jim. "She's either the smartest woman or the dumbest woman in the world," he remarked.

While they were guessing about me in Ann Arbor, I sat with Daddy in the hospital, eagerly watching him bounce back from major surgery even at age seventy-one. Mother relaxed and slept better just knowing that I was there. I did some reading and wrote letters while Daddy rested, but I longed to get back to work.

A stack of mail a mile high confronted me when I got back to my apartment in Columbus. Flipping hastily through the pile, I spied a letter that was postmarked Ann Arbor.

Who would be writing me from Ann Arbor? I don't know anyone there, I puzzled. It was a small envelope of personal stationery, obviously not a business letter. To satisfy my curiosity, I decided I would open just this one before I fell into bed.

One quick scan left me breathless. Jim Reapsome was writing to ask if we could write to each other and look for opportunities to get better acquainted.

"Look for opportunities to get better acquainted. . . . Coming from a widower with two young children, that's no casual request." It might as well have been midday. My drowsiness and fatigue fled. Millions of questions bombarded my mind.

Suddenly I remembered what I had thought when I first heard about Jim's grief. *What if you're the one to help meet his needs?* I had responded then, "Lord, if this thought is from you, you speak to Jim about it."

Wow! It looked suspiciously as if God had done just that while I had been totally oblivious to what was happening. A

5

few days later, after much prayer and soul searching, I nervously answered Jim's letter. Yes, I was interested in getting better acquainted.

Jim chose Good Friday—an appropriate day, I thought—for our first date in Columbus. I was as eager, anxious, and excited as a little girl anticipating her third birthday party. No pin-the-tail-on-the-donkey games for us, though. We planned a leisurely candlelight dinner at the Lincoln Lodge. My only disappointment: the wonderful evening ended all too soon. I think we could have talked all night.

I floated into the apartment, bumping my head on the ceiling. Smiling knowingly, my roommates asked all the right questions. About 2:00 A.M. I was calming down enough to go to bed. Just then we heard shouts from the street where Jim had parked his car. Quickly turning off the lights, we looked to see a car speeding away. Had someone stolen his car? We didn't know if he had driven or walked to nearby friends.

What should I do? Should I call him at this hour just to be sure?

In sheer agony I decided to call. If his car had been stolen, it would be better to know it now and notify the police. If it hadn't, at least he'd know I cared.

My friend Pete answered in a sleepy, irritated voice. "Jim Reapsome? Yes, he's here. Wait a minute." Too chicken, I didn't even identify myself.

Haltingly, I confessed the episode to Jim. "You wonder if someone stole my car? No, I didn't leave it there. I drove over here," he mumbled in disbelief. Relieved and embarrassed, I apologized for waking him.

How different this first date was from one that I'd had in college. That fellow hadn't impressed me enough for me to make the effort to remember his name. But tonight I had awakened friends at 2:30 A.M. for Jim Reapsome's protection.

Two other eventful dates showed me how this man handled unexpected crises. Jim made several trips from Chicago to Philadelphia, by way of Columbus, of course. His train conveniently arrived from the West about 8:00 A.M. and left for the East about 7:00 P.M. That meant we could have an all-day date between trains. Unorthodox, but fun.

The first time I met the morning train, I watched and waited as the passengers tramped up the stairs. The crowd thinned out. Still no Jim. Was I being stood up? Had he missed the train? Had I misunderstood the day?

Disappointment surged through my heart but quickly evaporated when he climbed into view at the top of the stairs with the conductor. They had been searching for his suitcase. Apparently, someone had mistakenly taken his suitcase; a similar bag had been left where Jim had put his. Patiently, he filled out a claim for his lost baggage, and we drove off hoping that the person who had made the mistake would eventually return his bag. But in the meantime, he would have to go to work in Philadelphia the next morning without being able to shave or to change clothes.

Our next date began handsomely. Train on time, suitcase safely stored in a station locker, we headed out of Columbus to stroll through a country garden resplendent in its full spring glory. Somehow, the flowers staged a uniquely brilliant show that matched our excitement in being together. We chatted over a cozy picnic lunch in a state park. To top off a perfect day, we decided on dinner in a small restaurant. The tables, adorned with red-and-white checked tablecloths and fresh flowers, spoke a gracious welcome. Comfortably relaxed, I

7

panicked when, in the middle of a sentence, Jim turned pale and began to reach into all his pockets.

"Are you all right?" I asked fearfully.

"I think I've lost the key to the locker in the station," he replied faintly.

After he searched every pocket the fourth time to no avail, we gulped down the rest of our meal and rushed to the station early. You won't believe how many papers you have to fill out and how many questions you have to answer to get the station master to open a locker. All this, twenty-five years before terrorist bombings. Unflustered, Jim endured the grilling until he got his suitcase barely four minutes before train time, so there were no lingering, fond farewells for us.

I had fumed and fidgeted impatiently over the lost suitcase and the lost key because they stole time from our dates. But Jim kept his cool and his courtesy throughout the delays. It takes mishaps like that to help develop a keen sense of what someone is made of.

During those agonizingly long weeks between our dates, Jim wrote faithfully, honestly, and openly. I avidly read each letter and learned what was important to him. His hunger for God stood out like a beacon. His sense of humor delighted me. His willingness to know me and have me know him drew me close to him.

The painstaking, demanding, and sometimes scary process of finding out what we were really like produced my confident "Yes!" on that Memorial Day in sparkling Schenley Park. My excitement and anticipation mounted as we planned our wedding. In Hazelwood United Methodist Church in Louisville, the following February, before our celebrating friends and families, we were married.

How my life changed! I thought about what would please Jim, not just what would please me. What would he like to eat or to do tonight? How would *we* spend *our* money, instead of how would *I* spend *my* money?

We never had enough time just to talk. I wanted to know everything about him, his childhood, his friends, his pets, where he'd lived, his dreams, all the sad and happy things that filled his memories. And I wanted him to know all that about me, too.

Our life together was to be for keeps, no strings attached. Our love and trust blossomed in a climate of mutual respect and openness. We truly wanted the best for each other.

Stories from the Journey

The relationship with my husband truly changed my life. It went from black and white to technicolor! His love for me helped me understand God's love better, especially the engagement ring. Since John and I were apart most of the six months we were engaged, there was something comforting and reassuring about that sparkling gem that caught the light and reminded me so often that *he loves me*. I was going through the grind of everyday classes, exams, work, financial worries . . . but all the time that ring reminded me that I was going to be *with him* in just a little while. I thought of how the Holy Spirit is like the engagement ring. The "guarantee of our inheritance," the first installment of all God plans to give. No matter what the

9

day holds, it catches the light and reminds us that he loves us and we will be with him.

Esther, 20s ∎

Just as I eagerly sought to know all I could about Jim before I married him, so I sought to learn about the Lord Jesus before I committed myself to him. That's how it is, too, with entering a woman's path to godliness.

Let me outline the basics, so at the outset we'll all be starting our journey with the same set of facts. In my search, I found that Jesus loves me so much that he left the glory of heaven to become a man, limited by a body, time, and space. He welcomed sinners; he had time for the people the world considered nobodies. He died in my place, for my sin. But he's alive in heaven praying for me. He offers me forgiveness and a place in God's family. And wonder of wonders, he wants my love and friendship much more than I want his. He's like a good shepherd searching for lost sheep. He's like a brave shepherd who willingly laid down his life for his sheep.

Gripped by the wonder of his love, I committed myself to him as my Savior and Lord at the same altar where, years later, I would commit myself to Jim as my husband. How my life changed after I boldly said, "I do," to Jesus! Now I think about what pleases Jesus, not just what pleases me. How can I live today with his approving smile? How can I show him my gratitude? How can I know him more intimately? What a stupendous relief that Jesus knows all the secrets of my heart and still wants the best for me. It's something like being in an airplane touching down on the runway after riding out a tumultuous descent through a thunderstorm.

God's best for me calls for change. He is making me like Jesus. Can you believe it? God is actually in the business of making everyone who joins his family by faith into the likeness of Jesus. That's what the path to godliness is all about.

In this book we'll explore this path that God walks with all his children. Certain mountain passes, crossroads, back streets, and narrow valleys lie in every person's path. For others, the path encompasses a cul-de-sac or two, a broad parade route, or a busy highway. God arranges a unique itinerary for every traveler along the path. Parts of the path I'll describe from my own exciting travels, other parts from my friends' astonishing pilgrimages, and some from the Bible's wonderful scenic views.

You can enter the path at any time, at any age, in any condition. Following the path to godliness will last a lifetime. Some days I feel discouraged at my slow, plodding pace. But a brief look over my shoulder to see how far I've already come spurs me on. Please join me on this adventure with God along the path to godliness.

Chapter Two

Good Morning, Lord

Along the way, thankfulness

A soupspoonful of chicken neck bones! "There are more bones than soup. I can't eat this," I wailed with all the disdain that a six-year-old could muster.

"Be thankful you have something to eat," Mother responded sharply.

I knew that she had brought the bones home from the hotel kitchen where she had worked as a cook since Daddy had broken his back while on a paperhanging job. Mother, his pasting helper, watched helplessly as the ladder holding the scaffolding in a third-floor stairway slipped, and Daddy tumbled to the bottom of the basement stairs.

Mother called Uncle Mac, an undertaker, to take Daddy and her to Dr. Rush's office. There they learned that Daddy had three cracked vertebrae. Knowing Daddy's patient disposition, and his lack of income or insurance, Dr. Rush let him go home to lie flat on his back for six weeks.

With a family of six to care for, Mother looked for work and became one of the cooks at a small hotel, the Nicholson, famous in Fern Creek, Kentucky, for its fried chicken. That house specialty produced lots of chicken necks and backs for the frugal cook trying to feed her family on her small salary. Time pressure didn't permit the luxury of removing all the neck bones from her nourishing chicken soup.

Mother's habit of finding reasons for thanksgiving rather than complaining began long before Daddy's accident. To be unthankful was a cardinal sin in her eyes. She took seriously God's diagnosis of the human problem: "For although they knew God, they neither glorified him as God *nor gave thanks to him,* but their thinking became futile and their foolish hearts were darkened" (Romans 1:21, italics added). If failure to give thanks was one step toward darkness, she wouldn't take that step.

Her thankfulness imprints my mind. Her singing filled the house: "What a Wonderful Savior Is Jesus My Lord"; "Praise Him, Praise Him"; "What a Friend We Have in Jesus"; "Amazing Grace"; "The Lily of the Valley." A thankful spirit accompanied the mindless tasks of housework.

She and Daddy repeatedly told us about God's provision for all our needs. Before they were married in 1917, they decided that their tithe would come out of the paycheck first each week. Then they would budget the rest. "Look at our house, clothes, and food. God has kept his promises," they loved to say. By any government study, we would have been classified as poor, but we had all we *needed.* Thankfulness was the proper response.

The last three years of her life, Mother was a semi-invalid. She dragged herself from her bed to a reclining chair in the living room. Cooking, which she loved more than anything else, became too difficult. Daddy or the housekeeper produced tasteless meals by her standards. Her three daughters lived hundreds of miles away. She couldn't worship in the second pew of Hazelwood Methodist Church, a spot she and Daddy had occupied for forty years.

But when friends visited her, she talked about the goodness of God. She recounted stories of his provision for her and her family. She told them to be thankful. She encouraged everyone who came to cheer her.

In April 1967, the doctor asked my brother to send for his sisters because Mother was weakening. For five days my sisters and I took turns sitting by Mother in the bedroom and sleeping in the single bed next to her rented hospital bed. My brother came as often as his business travels permitted. Sometimes, just after Mother had her pain medication, we all sat together laughing over memories and just enjoying the rare privilege of being together. When Mother was restless, one of us would sit close to hold her hand and listen if she wanted to talk.

Because of his deafness, Daddy had put a yardstick in Mother's bed each night so she could reach over to his bed and poke him if she needed help. He looked exhausted when my sisters and I arrived. With great relief, he moved to the basement for nights of uninterrupted sleep. The doctor hadn't told us yet that he was treating Daddy for what turned out to be bladder cancer.

The first day as I sat holding her thin, gnarled hand, Mother asked me, "Do you think I've been guilty of the sin of unthankfulness?"

I could hardly believe her question. After all the years of living and speaking gratitude, she feared being unthankful.

"Mother, whatever you may be guilty of, it isn't unthankfulness," I assured her. She seemed to rest more quietly after that. I wondered how my thankfulness rated on a scale of one to ten. At that moment, it looked like a two.

On the fifth evening my sisters and I were there, after Daddy had gone to bed, Mother surprised us by asking us to gather around her bed to pray together. In spite of her weakness, she spoke firmly and confidently. She thanked God for the Lord Jesus, his dying for her and forgiving her. She thanked him for her family. As we clung on every word, I heard only one request: "Lord, may my whole family be faithful to Christ and may we all be reunited in heaven—everyone."

"Let's sing," she said and began without a quiver in her voice, "What a Wonderful Savior Is Jesus My Lord." Recovering from surprise, we followed her lead and struggled to sing through our tears. "Now you each choose a hymn," she directed. We tried, but the words of the hymns "Rock of Ages," "My Jesus, I Love Thee," and "What a Friend We Have in Jesus" barely left our lips.

Exhausted, she rested back on the pillows. "That's all I can sing now." After a pause, "Now what do we do? Just lie down and wait for the wagon?" Her eyes closed and she slept peacefully. It seemed to me that she had pronounced her own benediction. It was all over. We sat motionless and stunned. Silence engulfed the room, but God unmistakably was there.

She awakened the next morning. Disappointment etched her face. It was as though she had expected to wake up in heaven instead of in her bed and in her painful body. She refused food and any medicine except painkillers. She just wanted to sleep away into the presence of the God she loved and to thank him face to face. Her desire was granted after five days in a coma.

Stories from the Journey

I thought I was being thankful because I regularly thanked God for all the good things in my life—the joys, blessings, and answers to prayer. But thank God for the pain? The difficult times? If I thank him for troubles, will he think I like them and give me more? It helps me to remember that growth came from my difficulties. Faith grew in winter.

JoAnn, 40s, mother of two ■

Thankfulness is a basic ingredient of godliness. Thankfulness is the appropriate response to God when I realize what he has done for me. "We are convinced that one died for all, and therefore all died. And he died for all, that those who live should no longer live for themselves but for him who died for them and was raised again" (2 Corinthians 5:14-15). Realizing Jesus' sacrifice makes me want to live all of life out of thankfulness to him.

Practicing thankfulness through my day might include saying the following: "Good morning, Lord. Thank you for a good night's sleep and a new day."

"Thank you for the clean, fresh taste in my mouth after I brush my teeth."

"Thank you for a parking place."

"Thank you for a sale on chicken this week."

"Thank you for reproving me for that jealous thought."

"Thank you for the cardinal on the snowy branch of the spruce tree."

"Thank you for giving Brahms such creative powers and for giving me the ability to hear and appreciate his music."

"Thank you for a day of rest in bed with a migraine. You know when I need to slow down."

"Thank you for resurrection lilies each August that remind me that resurrection is a reality."

"Thank you for the foxglove blooming against the fence. Effortlessly it stands in place glorifying you."

"Thank you for keeping me from going on the defensive when Gene accused me of selfish motives."

"Thank you for Jim's laughter as he reads *Lake Wobegon Days*."

"Thank you for a phone call from a neighbor who wants to be a friend."

"Thank you for the letter from Sally and your comforting her in her deep sorrow."

Mother's example encourages me to obey the command to give thanks in *all* circumstances, desirable and undesirable (see 1 Thessalonians 5:18). Anyone can be thankful when everything is fine. Giving thanks for pain and uncertainty pushes me to trust God's goodness when I don't feel it.

Chapter Three

No Ifs, Ands, or Buts about It

Along the way, trust

It's heartrending to watch your mother die. For five days, Mother talked with us and ate a little, but she was tired and eager to die. For years she had asked God to spare her from being an invalid, dependent on others. But her family was drawn from across the country to care for her in her last days. Inside, I bled deeply for her. Her helplessness was as anguishing as her physical pain. After she prayed with us that fifth night, her being alive frustrated her even more.

I would sit with her for a while, but my utter helplessness drove me upstairs to cry and scream at God, "Can't you take her today? Must she wake up another day still here? Please be merciful and take her home."

Mercy, perhaps, brought a coma. Five more days ground by at a snail's pace. We kept vigil, but we were spared Mother's questioning eyes. Finally, her life ebbed quietly away. Relief and comfort flooded my soul because Mother was free at last. Like a butterfly struggling free from the cocoon, Mother was free in the presence of Christ. I was glad. Yes, glad in the presence of death, because Jesus, the resurrection and the life, promised, "He who believes in me will live, even though he dies; and whoever lives and believes in me will never die" (John 11:25-26).

Meanwhile, back in Philadelphia, Jim's weekly Christian newspaper, *The Sunday School Times,* was sold. That was the end of his six-year stint as editor of the venerable 108-year-old institution. At the same time, John, our six-year-old son, developed mysterious leg pains. He refused to walk. Uncle Ed and Aunt Betty, who were caring for Sara and John in my absence, carried him home from school. The doctor thought he had phlebitis.

Mother prayed to die but lingered on. Jim suffered the shock and depression of losing the paper into which he had poured his heart and talents. A little boy cried in pain, and no one could help him.

The news from home pulled me apart. I cried, "Lord, do you have your timing mixed up? How can you allow all these things at the same time? Everyone needs me today. I want to be with Jim and John and Mother all at the same time. I don't think I can cope with all this at once." No answers came from voices in the sky, but God was there. I knew that he heard and, most of all, that he cared. Troubled, but not gripped with anxiety, I flew back to Philadelphia after the funeral.

I went home to comfort my husband and my son. Jim and I both needed comfort and support, him for the loss of his job, and me for the loss of my mother. For the first time in our marriage, severe crises attacked us both at the same time. Fear nosed its way into my consciousness. We were spent emotionally and had little to give each other.

John's illness demanded our attention first. Our pediatrician ran him through a battery of tests. More office visits. More blood samples and x-rays. We had to rush back and forth like a team of paramedics because the doctor needed to examine John when he was hurting. When John cried or refused to walk, that was the emergency signal. Quickly carry him to the car. Drive five miles across town to the doctor's office. Park as close to the door as possible. Lug John up the steps into the office. By then the leg pains usually had stopped, and John wanted to go home to play. Was he playing games with us? Was our emotional turmoil affecting John?

Getting a diagnosis can be both a relief and a terror. Finally, the test results showed that John had rheumatoid arthritis. At last we knew he really was sick. But thoughts of a boy crippled for life chilled us like the blast of a subzero gale. To prevent permanent joint damage, John had to go to bed for six weeks. He could not put any weight on his legs. We moved him into the first-floor bedroom. Like soldiers on guard duty, we regularly carried him to the bathroom and back. Games and toys poured in from our friends. His little room looked like F.A.O. Schwarts toy store at Christmas time. Such love not only brought tears to our eyes but also sparked many happy hours of game playing.

It was too late in May to get a home tutor. The load piled higher on me. I felt like the Israelites in Egypt forced to gather their own straw to make bricks while maintaining their previous production level. In addition to keeping John pacified in bed and happily entertained, I also had to teach him the last six weeks of his first-grade work. Tremblingly, I trudged up the hill to his school. I can still see his class of healthy, busy children working at their desks. As I got John's books and materials from his teacher, terrifying doubt seized me. I wondered when, and if, John would ever be able to be part of a regular classroom again. Would permanent bone damage keep him from playing at recess? The teacher droned on about the schoolwork to cover, but it was all a blur, shrouded in the mists of my tears and fears.

Jim's job search turned up nothing. Promising doors opened, only to slam shut. Should he continue in journalism? Should he go for another degree? What was God trying to say to us? Many nights as we collapsed into bed, it was all we could do to cling to each other and pray. "Pray without ceasing" meant a constant "Help! Help!"

My body was the first to protest. "Overload!" it shrieked in the form of frequent and severe migraine headaches. One day a man came to town to interview Jim for a job, so we invited him to dinner. Although it was the first meal I'd prepared for company since returning from Mother's funeral about six weeks before, it was no big deal. A simple supper for five. *Piece of cake,* I thought. How wrong I was. Deeply chagrined, I realized as we sat down that I'd forgotten to make a salad. At any other time, salad would have been a routine matter. My life had become a desert, wider and drier than any I'd ever crossed before.

God eventually opened a door for Jim. He became chaplain at Malone College, Canton, Ohio, and taught Bible and journalism. He found it exciting, challenging, and demanding to work with students again. However, loneliness engulfed me. I left behind my friends in the neighborhood Bible study group. They had faithfully stood by me in the desert months. My new neighbors and the faculty wives didn't know about my recent bouts with grief, fear, and uncertainty. Those aren't things to casually discuss with strangers.

God's healing, nevertheless, worked. By September, we knew that John had suffered no permanent joint damage. Gradually, the grief of Mother's death lessened. Jim's excitement at Malone spilled over onto me. The hot dog roasts with students stacked into our house lifted my spirit like a shower after a day of sweaty toil in the garden. What had God been up to in the past months? Could we see his footprints in the dry desert?

In the months before Jim and I were married, I had been studying the book of Isaiah. One of the prophet's dire warnings and dramatic promises struck me:

If only you had paid attention to
    my commands,
your peace would have been
    like a river,
your righteousness like the waves
    of the sea.
They did not thirst when he led
    them through the deserts;

he made water flow for them
from the rock;
he split the rock
and water gushed out.

Isaiah 48:18, 21

In my prayer journal I had written: "Father, I claim this experience for Jim and me. When you lead us through deserts, we will not thirst. You will make water flow from rocks, even gush out. May we so obey your commands that you can give us peace like a river and righteousness like waves of the sea."

Now, years later, I reread what I had written in that special notebook. Not every day, but often, I record an idea God impresses on me from my Bible reading and my response to it. Other days I just pour out my fears, joys, hopes, desires, whatever I want to say to God. Rereading the prayers of years before usually startles me, as I see my life today in light of what I asked of God.

I realized that God had given us water in those four desert months. In the desert, we had drunk from the gushing stream and known peace like a river. Sometimes a cool drink came from a friend who brought warm raisin muffins or a new game for John or from the friend who came to cut John's hair. But the gushing, refreshing streams came from sitting quietly in God's presence, reading and rereading his promises and his faithfulness to people in the past. As I focused on God, the River Peace flowed through my desert. God had done just what he had said he would do. My experience told me that I could trust him.

Stories from the Journey

My major lesson in trust came through following God when it was unpopular with my family and closest friends for me to do so. I grew up depending heavily on my family. Through high school I enjoyed their loving support. When I decided to join a Christian drama group for a year, they cheered my unconventional choice and prayerfully sent me off.

Learning to communicate the gospel through drama in schools, parks, churches, and cafeterias stretched my faith, sharpened my skills, and confirmed my gifts. Confident God had put me in this demanding but joyful ministry, I committed myself to the group for longer and longer lengths of time and as far away as South Africa.

Doubts and questions about my ministry poured out of my family and friends like water spewing from a ruptured main. I struggled to do what I felt the Lord was calling me to do when those I love the most withdrew their support. But out of the struggles, I began to see more clearly who God is, who I am, and why I believe in him. The Lord began to transfer my dependence from my family to himself. Eventually, by obeying and trusting God, I earned the confidence of my family again. But the issue for me is to depend on God when he directs another unpopular choice.

Linda, 30s, mother of one ■

Learning to trust someone takes time, time to get to know the individual. That's the way it was with Dr. Fisher. We had

25

just moved to town. You know what it's like. Finding a doctor and a dentist can be the hardest part of moving. I went to see Dr. Fisher because several neighbors recommended him.

A short, stout, partly bald man smiled warmly when he introduced himself and shook my hand. He asked about our family and what had brought us to East Petersburg. We discussed the town's good points and agreed we were glad to live there. Then he asked why I had come to see him. He listened carefully as I recited my symptoms, interrupting only to ask a question or two. After the examination, he explained his diagnosis, gave me a packet of medicine, and wished me well. I felt better already, even without the medicine, because Dr. Fisher had taken me seriously. He had listened to me and cared about me as a person. I wasn't just another patient paying a fee.

Needless to say, he became a firm friend as well as our family physician. We learned to know Dr. Fisher, to appreciate his help, and to trust him.

That's what it's like to learn to trust God. I need information about him to trust him. That's what my Bible study is all about. Sometimes it's hard for me actually to believe that God wants me to know what he is like. But he does—no ifs, ands, or buts about it.

I became a Christian as a teenager, but I didn't know how to study the Bible. I needed help. I tried to read the Bible daily, but because I couldn't understand it, I would quit. That was no good because guilt overwhelmed me and I would start again. I repeated the cycle until the spring of my freshman year in college. Then a remarkable thing happened that revolutionized my life.

A group of us from Western Kentucky University packed up in our cars and drove to an Inter-Varsity Christian Fellowship weekend conference in southern Indiana. Speaking to us was a cheerful, spunky woman named Jane Hollingsworth who was originally from the South but now lived in the North. We liked this woman. On Saturday afternoon she held a Bible study clinic. Wow! You could hear minds blowing all over the place. Using the story about the sinful woman who interrupted the Pharisee's dinner party to anoint Jesus' feet with perfume (see Luke 7:36-50), Jane dramatized it for us in the first person. We were there. Jane was that woman. Suddenly the Bible became alive. Real people breathed, cried, scoffed, and laughed in the Bible.

As Jane spoke, I saw the woman slip quietly into the room and kneel behind Jesus as he reclined at the table. She brought an alabaster jar of perfume, but before she could open it, she began to weep. Jesus' feet were wet with her tears. What should she do? She removed the pins from her hair, letting it fall over his feet. She began kissing his feet as she wiped them with her hair. Imagine what it must have felt like to be the only woman in that room full of men, all staring at her and scorning her.

I was humiliated with her. Her desperation to get to Jesus became mine. Her remorse over her sin, her willingness to risk rejection, her relief at Jesus' words, "Your sins are forgiven," and her joy at his statement, "Your faith has saved you: go in peace," all of her emotional wrenchings clamped my heart like a vise.

I'd never heard anything like this before. In this story Jesus was a living person. He reached out to real people with emotions like mine. If I put myself in their skin and thought about what they felt, the conversations on the page rang with their feelings, even with the tones of their voices. A new resolve seized me. No, it was more like hunger for roast beef, potatoes, and carrots. If God could speak to Jane Hollingsworth like that, he could speak to me as well.

Armed with the study guides that Jane had written on the Gospel of Mark and 1 Peter—plus a notebook and an alarm clock, to get me up a half-hour earlier—I began to find out for myself what Jesus was really like. Years had passed since I had committed myself to him, but for all practical purposes, he was still a stranger—like someone met once at a party and then forgotten. I wasn't sure how much I could trust him.

What kind of a person did this stranger, Jesus, turn out to be? I was struck by his intensely personal touch. When Jesus healed a leper, he touched him (see Mark 1:40-45). Jesus had healed other people with just a word, but he chose to touch the leper. Why? I thought, *What a touch must mean to a man who hadn't been able to hug his wife and children; to a man who had to cry, "Unclean, unclean," so people wouldn't accidentally touch him.* Jesus' touch healed the leper's heart as well as his body. Jesus can make me whole emotionally and physically.

One day Jesus was interrupted in the middle of a sermon in a jam-packed house when a paralyzed man was lowered through the roof (see Mark 2:1-11). Jesus didn't blow his top. With magnificent self-composure, he first forgave and then healed the man. The helpless man was more important than the sermon, the roof, or the opinion of the scribes in the audience who criticized Jesus for claiming to be able to forgive sins. Surely Jesus cares about my need to be forgiven. He isn't too busy to notice me and my faith, even though he is the Lord of the universe.

What about the woman who slipped through the crowd and touched the hem of Jesus' cloak because she wanted to be healed (see Mark 5:25-34)? She had been hemorrhaging for twelve years. By the law, she was unclean and shouldn't have been in the crowd. Jesus stopped at her touch and asked the person who had touched him to step forward. At first, his question seemed very cruel to me. That poor woman certainly didn't want to stand in front of all those people and tell her story.

But Jesus didn't want to let her go home with just the little she had asked for. He forced her to identify herself, not to embarrass her, but to send her home with peace and to commend her for her faith.

That's how I saw that Jesus wants to do more for me than I ask for. He understands much better than I do what I really need. He saves each of us from running away with just a part of what we need.

Remember when the disciples returned from a preaching trip and Jesus suggested that they take a day off (see Mark 6:31)? Maybe they were just exhausted from traveling and constantly giving to people. Maybe they needed time to talk and to hear about everything that had happened. I don't know exactly what they needed, but I do know that Jesus understands my physical and emotional needs for rest.

Before Jesus was arrested, he knew that Peter would turn traitor and deny him (see Mark 14:30-38). Yet Jesus patiently and tenderly warned Peter, encouraged him to pray, and continued to share His own deep sorrow. After the Resurrection, Jesus took Peter for a walk for a private reconciliation (see

John 21:15-25). He gave Peter a second chance, despite his dismal failure. I'm thankful for every fresh start Jesus has given me.

Since Jesus is the same today as he was yesterday and he will be forever, I can trust him. He is gentle and patient. He forgives me, corrects me, and restores me. As he was with people then, so I can trust him to be with me now.

Chapter Four

The Thrill of Discovery

Along the way, personal Bible study

I got excited about studying the Bible because Jane Hollings-worth exuded the thrill of her own discoveries. Since then, I've discovered some valuable tools that will work for you, too. Simple and easy to use, these tools are just like a trusty garden fork and a trowel. You can dig deeply with them and uncover God's marvelous treasures. As you do, your heart and soul will be warmly enriched.

Jesus said an amazing thing: "I praise you, Father, Lord of heaven and earth, because you have hidden these things from the wise and learned, and revealed them to little children. Yes, Father, for this was your good pleasure" (Matthew 11:25-26).

Because our Father loves to show special things to his children, I need to jump into his lap, so to speak, with all the eager anticipation of a two-year-old. Children love to bombard parents with questions. Study guides with good questions worked best for me.

For personal study, my favorite is *This Morning with God,* edited by Carol Adeney. If you want to learn to write your own questions, I recommend *The Joy of Discovery in Bible Study* by Oletta Wald.

What are the key questions that will give us insights into and instructions from God's Word? In many ways they are just like the questions our kids ask us. First, there are fact questions: Who? Where? When? What? How?

Who is here? Who is speaking to whom?

Where are they?

When is this happening?

What is happening?

How is this happening?

Second, there are meaning questions: How? Why? How does this paragraph fit with the ones before and after it? How does the dictionary define that word? What did this mean to the person to whom it was said or written?

Third, there are application questions: What difference does this make to me today? How does this open up some new understanding of God? Is there an example to follow or one to avoid? Is there a promise to claim? Is there a command to obey? What is my prayer from this passage?

I'm glad that I was introduced to Bible study when I was a college student. Since I had learned to keep a notebook and a pen handy so that I could record my thoughts and take notes from what I was reading, I easily transferred this study habit to my Bible study. I got so excited about my Bible discoveries that I could hardly wait until I graduated. You see, I thought my college schedule was so full that I would have lots more time for Bible study after college. How wrong I was! At least I had a schedule in college. I could write in my daily appointment with God along with History 203. But after college, my orderly framework collapsed. Schedules became more fluid or nonexistent. How could I, a mother with a baby and a preschooler, keep a regular pattern of personal Bible study? Only with careful discipline and budgeting of time. It has to be written into my schedule. Knowing that God wants to meet with me helps, too.

Stories from the Journey

 Personal study helps:

1. A Bible I can mark up—underline key words, circle connectives, bracket comparisons, etc.
2. Different-colored highlighters—promises one color, commands another, etc.
3. Wide margins in which to write definitions
4. Several standard translations on hand to compare
5. Reading slowly
6. Asking myself questions:
    - What do I learn about God here?
    - What is God telling me to do?
    - Of what is the Holy Spirit convicting me?
    - What is my prayer from this passage?

Esther, 20s ■

What happens on days when I don't read the Bible? That old bugaboo guilt attacks me again. I wonder if I can just start over, pretending that I haven't neglected God. Obviously, the accuser says, I've got to make myself miserable for a while. I've got to flagellate myself for my failure, like the desert fathers used to do. Then I can start reading the Bible again.

What lies! When the child stumbles, the parent doesn't say, "Lie there, you failure." No, the parent patiently encourages the toddler to get up and try again. I've learned to admit my failure and start again. It's just like falling off a bicycle when you're trying to learn to ride. You get up and start peddling as fast as you can because the thrill of the ride is worth it.

Missing a day of Bible study doesn't defeat me. Neither does a dull study time. I've learned to persist when Bible study is mundane. It isn't always exciting. Some days no bells ring, no lights flash.

Studying the Bible is a lot like storing food. When I lug in five heavy grocery bags, I put some food in the freezer, some in the refrigerator, and some in the cabinets. I don't cook everything I bought; I cook only what I need for the next meal. I'll take other items out of storage tomorrow or the following day, as I need them.

My daily study time enables me to store the Bible in my heart. I may not see how I need what I'm reading now, but by storing it away, I'll be able to pull it out when I do need it later on—today or tomorrow or some other day.

For example, while writing this book, I've been crying out to God every day, "I need wisdom. I'm not wise enough to write this book. I don't know what the reader needs. Please, give me your wisdom." Imagine what I found in my storage cabinet: "You are in Christ Jesus, who has become for us wisdom from God" (1 Corinthians 1:30). Years ago I studied those ideas in 1 Corinthians about wisdom. Today that stored food is just what I need.

God says that the Bible is one of the chief tools he uses to make us like the Lord Jesus: "All Scripture is God-breathed and is useful for teaching, rebuking, correcting and training in righteousness, so that the man of God may be thoroughly equipped for every good work" (2 Timothy 3:16-17). Think how much we need teaching and training in righteousness: positive input of information and practice in using it. Let me share one experience to show how this principle works.

Just before Jim and I were married, I was studying the book of Romans. When I tried to apply Paul's prayer for the church to marriage, a whole new cluster of ideas suddenly blossomed. Here's his prayer: "May the God of steadfastness and encouragement grant you to live in such harmony with one another, in accord with Christ Jesus, that together you may with one voice glorify the God and Father of our Lord Jesus Christ" (Romans 15:5-6, RSV).

Thinking about harmony in marriage, I realized that it requires the sensitive blending of two voices, neither dominating the other. Jim and I would have to learn to do that. Second, we'd certainly need steadfast encouragement from God and from each other. Third, our learning to become one voice had the potential of glorifying God. Well, that started something. The more Jim and I talked and prayed, the more we thought about having Romans 15:5-6 inscribed in our wedding bands. So we did just that.

Also during our engagement, I was anxiously anticipating how Sara and John would take to me, especially three-year-old Sara. How could I win her love? Would she see me as a threat? Would she be jealous?

God spoke to those intensely personal needs. I found the teaching I needed in 1 John 4:19: "We love because he first

35

loved us." Think of it—people love in return for love they receive! I love God because he first loved me. So, if Sara could sense and receive love from me, she could learn to love me in return. From that day, I began to pray, "Lord, help me so to love Sara that she will feel loved and be completely convinced that I really do love her."

Stories from the Journey

 When my best friend accused me of abandonment, I felt like I had been hit in the stomach. I thought I'd never breathe again. What pain to be misunderstood, to have my good intentions hurt the person I love. As I wrestled with anger, self-pity, and depression, I neglected my only source of help—time alone with God. When I restored my daily quiet time with God, listening to him from the Bible and the Holy Spirit, peace returned. The situation remained unchanged. But I changed.

Marian, 30s ■

In addition to teaching and training, we also need the Bible for rebuking and correcting. Here's how this principle worked for my friend Chris. She and her husband, Dan, had been having serious problems ever since he had returned from military service in Germany. She had been complaining about Dan to the women she worked with at the bank. They gave her unqualified sympathy and zeroed in on Dan's weaknesses.

Chris began to consider separation, until one morning when she read Psalm 1:1:

> *Blessed is the man*
> *who does not walk in the counsel of*
> *the wicked*
> *or stand in the way of sinners*
> *or sit in the seat of mockers.*

Like a shot from an arrow aimed right at her heart, God's Word rebuked and corrected her. She had been walking in the counsel of the wicked. She had not asked counsel from God or from fellow Christians. God was graciously doing what he said he would do: use the Bible to lead us along the path to godliness.

As a little child continually discovering her world, I want to keep exploring God's treasures. Even on the days that don't yield diamonds, I store away what the Holy Spirit can use to teach and correct me.

Chapter Five

Three Mothers and the Master Teacher

Along the way, neighborhood
Bible study

As I write in the spring, the luscious vegetables and gorgeous flowers in the Miracle-Gro commercials fill our TV screen. That fertilizer's ingredients will turn everyone's thumb green. Miracle-Gro for my spiritual fruit is a handful of friends studying the Bible regularly with me. My confidence in God blooms like the most spectacular roses because of what he has done for me and my neighbors through Bible study.

Every time we move (which, by the way, has been four times in the thirty years we've been married), I can hardly wait to meet my new neighbors and tell them about Bible study. Those first few months waiting for the opportunities to ripen are the hardest for me.

It all began in 1962 with Betty, who lived next door, and Alice, across the street, and me. The instruction book I had ordered *(How to Start a Neighborhood Bible Study,* by Marilyn Kunz and Catherine Schell) said that we should start with four to nine people. If any of the women had children, we were supposed to hire a baby sitter.

There were only three of us, but I couldn't wait any longer, rules or no rules. I had been praying for months for a group like this. Betty's husband objected to having a sitter, so contrary to the rules of good group dynamics, we started: three mothers with three preschoolers, meeting each Wednesday at 10:00 A.M. to study the Gospel of Mark. We took turns asking the questions and moved from home to home, week by week. This was no coffee klatch, but a real, honest-to-goodness Bible study.

Betty was a young, petite redhead. Although her church was important to her, she had never examined her faith or talked about it. In Mark 3 we read about Jesus casting out demons. The Jewish religious leaders accused him of being possessed by the devil. Jesus replied that no one could plunder a strong man's house until he had first tied up the strong man. Suddenly Betty beamed. She exclaimed, "That means my Friend is stronger than my enemy. I don't have to be afraid."

Depending on Jesus' love and power, Betty began to change. One day she told us that she was teaching her daughter to pray. Not long after—under Betty's persuasion—her pastor started a women's Bible study, using his Scripture reading for the following Sunday. When Terry, her husband, pursued agnosticism, Betty refused to panic.

We both moved away, but years later we rediscovered each other in nearby towns. The news wasn't good. In fact, life had taken an ugly turn for Betty. She was thin and worn. Terry had divorced her. Their unwed teenage daughter had a baby and was struggling with being a single parent. Out of their hurt and anger over the divorce, the other two children rebelled.

As we talked and cried together over lunch, Betty painfully described her troubles. But her honesty was accompanied by a gentle, quiet spirit. There wasn't a trace of bitterness. God had comforted her. My grasp of God's goodness and faithfulness grew bigger and bigger, thanks to her peace in the center of a storm.

Betty decided she wanted to be a hospital chaplain. She went back to college and is now in seminary. How delighted she is to be studying the Gospel of John in Greek! Where did her path to godliness begin? In our little Bible study group, where she met Jesus.

Stories from the Journey

 I stay in the neighborhood Bible study because they listen to me. Growing up the youngest of seven children meant nobody listened to me. On my first visit to the group, I remember how they looked at me when I spoke and really listened. We've studied Mark, Acts, and 1 Corinthians. About the middle of Acts I had assurance that I have spiritual life in Jesus Christ.

In 1 Corinthians I learned two important facts: (1) I won't be tempted beyond my strength. (2) I am a new creation in Christ Jesus, not just patched up, but new.

Margaret, 30s, mother of two ∎

Women often regard me with a perplexed look when I tell them how satisfying Bible study can be with their neighbors. By now I know what to expect. "How can this work without a teacher?" they ask. It works because God is the teacher. As the master teacher, he knows what each one of us is ready to learn. He knows how fast each one of us can absorb new ideas.

When I started our first group, I was so afraid that I wouldn't know the right answers. My neighbors wouldn't learn the truth, and it would be all my fault. Then God rebuked me. It was as though he said, "Who do you think you are? Whose study is this anyway? I'll be the teacher." What a relief! I relaxed as a fellow learner and watched God teach me and my friends.

Stories from the Journey

 I tried to read the Bible, but I didn't understand it. When Mary invited me to join a study, I came reluctantly because I knew so little. But the questions helped us find answers in Mark. We actually studied the whole Gospel of Mark, and I understood it!

Cathy, 30s, mother of two ∎

Let me tell you about Lois, a self-confident yet reserved, well-educated professional teacher with two children. She brought a ton of questions to our group. In college she had been well schooled in all the reasons why the Bible can't be trusted. But when she heard that we, her neighbors, simply wanted to discover what the Bible had to say, she joined us. She figured it was time to learn what it says, and besides, she was hungry for God.

One day we read how Jesus answered the Sadducees, who said there is no resurrection: "Now about the dead rising—have you not read in the book of Moses, in the account of the bush, how God said to him, 'I am the God of Abraham, the God of Isaac, and the God of Jacob'? He is not the God of the dead, but of the living" (Mark 12:26-27). Instantly relief broke across Lois's face. Then she exclaimed, "There is life after death. I've never been sure."

We didn't know it at the time, but Lois's father had died a few months before our group began to meet. She feared there was no life after death. None of us could have made the specific application that she needed out of that verse. But God knew what Lois needed, and he taught her that day.

A few months later, Lois brightly announced to us, "I've stopped working on the things I don't believe. Now I'm working on what I do believe." What was going on? I hadn't given her a lot of intellectual data. God had convinced her of his truth. I could never have done that, but he did. God is the superlative Teacher. You can make that discovery, too, if you allow him to meet you and your friends in Bible study.

Another common question I hear is, "But do people actually come to faith in Christ in these groups?" Yes, many do. Take Sue, for example, a young mother in suburbia, busy with her family, with no need or time for church. She had been in a group for only a few months before she had to move. But later she wrote to her old neighbors, "I'm so glad I was in the Bible study while you studied Acts, because I learned what a Christian is, and I became one."

Stories from the Journey

 God gave me a dramatic lesson in not deciding who to invite to Bible study. Four years ago, when I invited neighbors to come for coffee to hear about the idea of a Bible study, I deliberately skipped Emily next door. I knew she wouldn't be interested because she had it all together. Her house was perfect. Her hair, her grooming, her clothes, her car, her career, her family were all perfect. She couldn't possibly have any sense of needing anything else in her life, it seemed to me.

But last summer, Emily kept coming to my mind every time I thought about the Bible study. God repeatedly nudged me to invite her in September. Reluctantly, I called to tell her the neighborhood Bible study would resume Tuesday morning and we'd love to have her visit to see if it interested her. To my utter amazement she came and came and came. After a few months, she stayed after the study one day, to thank me for inviting her to the study. "I didn't think anyone cared, and I was contemplating suicide," she confided.

Lucy, 40s, mother of three ■

God draws people to himself even when they aren't aware of it. Strange how something like this often works. Diana asked me to a coffee with her neighbors. That's how neighborhood Bible study groups usually start—people come for coffee and listen to someone tell about the idea.

After I explained what a Bible study involves, we studied a paragraph from the Gospel of Mark. Then I asked, "Who thinks this is interesting enough to give it a try?"

A young woman named Jenny had eagerly accepted Diana's invitation to the coffee, although the two barely knew each other. She was the first to respond to my invitation. Waving the study guide in her hand, she said excitedly, "I want to join. I want to know what the Bible says. I tried reading the Old Testament and couldn't understand it, so I quit. I started reading the New Testament, but I couldn't understand it, so I quit. I want to be in a Bible study."

Then I recall what happened on one city block. Heather, a new bride who had recently moved into the neighborhood, stepped out with courageous faith. She went door to door inviting her neighbors to a coffee to hear about the idea of a Bible study. No one was home at the first house. At the second house, the woman closed the door with a firm, "No thanks." Weakening, Heather questioned, "Lord, is this the right idea or the right place?" To find out, she tried one more house. Marti opened the door, and Heather told her about the coffee. To Heather's amazement, Marti eagerly invited her in. "I've wanted to join a Bible study, but I didn't know how," she said. "My sister is in a study group in another town and loves it. She keeps telling me how great it is."

Both Jenny and Marti soaked up the Bible like dry sponges. They soon found God and realized that he had been pursuing them all along.

Stories from the Journey

 I counted up all the things I was doing for my family: changing hems, cooking, shopping, chauffeuring, being a den mother, library volunteer, etc., etc. But I decided that the best thing I could do for my family was to develop my spiritual life. That's why I stay in Bible study.

Helen, 30s, mother of four ■

I wish everyone could be in a Bible study group with people looking for God, with neighbors or friends or fellow workers who are new to the Bible. They may be in your block, or they may be the people you work with. They may be your bowling team or the moms of the Tuesday preschool. Resist the temptation to prejudge who might be or might not be interested in studying the Bible. You may have a Jenny or a Marti in your neighborhood. I hope you are in the Bible study with them when they find God.

Chapter Six

Only God Can Hug and Kiss You Inside

Along the way, self-worth

We all stood around the coffeepot one Sunday morning, chatting as we usually do before class. We weren't talking about anything in particular, just making small talk. "How's it going?" "Fine." That sort of thing.

Suddenly, as if someone had thrown a bomb into the room, Ginger answered my innocuous question—"How's your week been?"—with an explosion of unaccustomed honesty. "I'm tired of trying to please people, to make them like me. I need a support place. Isn't there anywhere I'm accepted just for me? I want someone to love me as I am."

I reeled in the aftereffects of her blast of candor. I felt the pain behind her words and wished I could wave a magic wand of acceptance over her. But before I could think of anything to say, she smiled and added, "I have that Person, don't I?"

Blinking back the tears, she went on, "I know God accepts me just as I am, but I need a daily reminder. I just don't have the discipline to have a regular quiet time for my personal devotions. I need to think of it not as a duty but as a time to let God love me. People can give you a hug and a kiss on the outside, but only God can hug and kiss you inside."

Trying to grasp her profound insights, I stayed with her as she explained further, "I tend to lean on people. But God keeps removing the people I want to lean on. Two years ago a friend helped me get a firmer grip on God's love. But that friendship has changed, and I can't go back there. I know God is asking me to lean on him."

Ginger's confession revealed that she knows the basic way to godliness. She knows that God accepts her, and she knows that he wants her to walk in bold dependence on him alone. But how can these biblical facts transform her spirit and her outlook on life? I'm sure her aspirations are shared by many of you. I see the answer in discovering one's self-worth before God.

Self-worth hinges not on pedigree, professional or home-making achievements, or even marital status. Three lies often seem to block the path to godliness: feelings of self-despair, feelings of incompetence, and feelings of incompleteness without a mate. Healthy self-worth, based on God's view of each of us in Christ, is the way to conquer all three.

The first lie that I had to conquer was feelings of self-despair. Probably the most revolutionary truth for me was the realization that since God had accepted me in Christ, I could therefore accept myself "warts and all," so to speak. I'll always remember how God got through to me about my self-worth. Day after day in July 1951, when I was a sophomore in college, I sat on the edge of the garbage pit at a Christian camp. Perched on a smooth rock, I read my Bible and prayed hard every morning. The rising sun streaming through the trees made even the vegetable peelings, bones, oatmeal, toast, and cake scraps shine. Behind me a foul-smelling wisp of smoke twisted toward the sky from the burn barrel.

At last I'd found a spot that matched my garbage-filled heart. For weeks, pride, deceitfulness, jealousy, envy, and evil thoughts had dominated my inner world and tormented my consciousness. If I did a kind deed or thought a humble thought, I was immediately proud of how virtuous or humble I was. More spiritual pride! More confession. I wept at the edge of the pit.

As I read my Bible and listened to the speakers that week, I heard God agreeing with me.

The heart is deceitful above
all things
and beyond cure.
Who can understand it?

Jeremiah 17:9

At least God wasn't surprised by what I was discovering about myself. My confessions held no new revelations for him. He was unshockable. But, like quicksand swallowing a helpless victim, the conviction of rottenness overwhelmed me.

One evening we started the service with a new hymn. I thought the writer, Charles Wesley, must have sat and pondered by a garbage pit just as I had. Anyway, he had discovered what I desperately needed to hear. These were the words that unlocked my chains:

And Can It Be That I Should Gain

And can it be that I should gain
An interest in the Saviour's blood?
Died he for me, who caused
   his pain?
For me, who him to death pursued?
Amazing love! how can it be
That thou, my God, shouldst die
   for me?

He left his Father's throne above,
So free, so infinite his grace,
Emptied himself of all but love,
And bled for Adam's helpless race.
Tis mercy all, immense and free;
for, O my God, it found out me!

No condemnation now I dread;
Jesus, and all in him, is mine!
alive in him, my living Head,
And clothed in righteousness divine,

Bold I approach th' eternal throne,
And claim the crown, through
Christ, my own.

At last I found my value and my inestimable worth. Yes, I am a sinner, but Jesus says I am worth dying for! By putting such a stupendous price tag on me, Jesus told me that I could honestly accept myself. This was no self-delusion. The burden floated away like so much chaff in the wind.

Stories from the Journey

 I identify with self-despair. I need radical transformation but fear the process, the feelings of loneliness, failure, and shame along the way. But when I remember to focus on the changes Christ has already produced in me, it's not so bad.

During my junior year of college, when God convicted me of a few particular sins, I responded by punishing myself and creating penance each time I repeated the sin. Finally, realizing I couldn't do the penance I had set for myself, I cried, "What's the use anyway?" After years of failing to meet God's standards by my own best efforts, I confessed to God: "I want to think I'm basically a good person, but I confess to you that I am a sinner." Grace flowed like high tide at full moon. I could breathe again. I was free, a sinner but forgiven.

I'm learning to discern conscience from the accuser. Conscience nudges me to positive actions like writing a cheery note, being on time, being diligent, considering the other person's feelings. The accuser shouts, "You failed. You're worthless. You can't. . . . You'll never learn . . . "

Esther, 20s ■

Worth and beauty, as the saying goes, are in the eyes of the beholder. At a household auction, an old cake plate was put up for bids. "Worthless junk," I sniffed. The milky white center was rimmed by a ragged blue border. "I wouldn't pay a dime for it," I whispered to Jim. "One hundred . . . two hundred," the auctioneer shouted. To my utter amazement, someone paid six hundred dollars for what was to me an ugly old plate. Never downplay your own value in God's eyes. It's the key to healthy self-worth.

The second lie I had to conquer in the path to godliness was the lie that self-worth depends on competence. If we're good at something, we say we must be worth something. In one sense, the disciples Jesus chose were a bunch of incompetents. But look what the Holy Spirit made of them. Their worth was determined not by how good they were but by what the Holy Spirit did in their lives.

Learning that my sense of competence comes from the Holy Spirit was a giant step along the path to godliness for me. His inexhaustible power and resources, not *my* abilities, produce competence. But I was slow to believe this. Here is how it happened.

During my summer break in 1955, while I was teaching school in Louisville, I joined other teachers and students in Ontario, Canada, to conduct vacation Bible schools in small churches. We were divided into teams and assigned to a church for two weeks. That's when I first spotted Doris. Without knowing her at all, I decided that she was the one person with whom I would not like to work. We were opposites in every way. She was the kind of person I carefully avoided.

But God had other plans. The bottom fell out of my stomach when Doris and I were assigned to the Dorset church. "Help! Help!" I cried to God. "I can't teach Bible school with her. I don't even like her. Her mannerisms irritate me." But I had to teach with her.

Frantically, I pleaded with God to make me love her, to fill me with love so she wouldn't know that I rejected her. Still, I thought she was a pest. I confessed that I couldn't love her, that I didn't even like her, but that I would truly try to love her. Sixty times an hour my frustrations ignited bitter cries for help.

For two weeks this incongruity dragged on—my loving Doris by sheer discipline but with no corresponding emotional feeling toward her. The day after Bible school finished, we gathered on the boat dock for our farewells. Awkwardly, I stared at my feet. Suddenly, Doris ran up and hugged me. She whispered, "I'm so glad we were assigned to teach together."

I nearly fell off the dock. The Holy Spirit had made Doris feel my love even when I didn't feel loving toward her. I had obeyed God the best I knew how, and the Holy Spirit made that enough. The Holy Spirit can produce his fruit, even in me! He loves to turn our incompetence into competence.

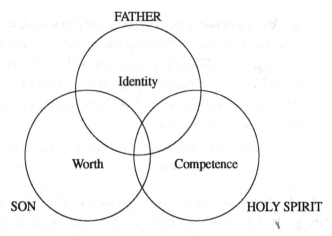

Our self-esteem is a reflection of the images the important people in our lives gave to us as children. Feeling accepted and valuable grew from statements like: "Sure, you can, just give it a try." "We're proud of you." "I know I can depend on you to do what is right." Feelings of rejection and incompetence grew from "Won't you ever learn?" "You're lazy." "Dummy." "Stringbean."

Don't despair if you grew up with only negative messages. You can collect new messages as an adult. Joann sings the praises of a friend who encouraged her.

Stories from the Journey

 You made me feel special. You always accepted me without criticism. That was something that never happened to me before. For the first time in my life I have self confidence. What a good feeling! Thanks for being there when I most needed a friend.

Your acceptance helped me change my idea of God. Instead of a harsh disciplinarian, God became the source of unconditional love. What joy when I discovered that God loves me as I am. I'm special. He loves me in spite of my imperfections. My self-confidence is still fragile like the tender seedlings in the spring, but it's growing.

Letter from Joann, 40s, mother of two, to her friend ■

God the Father gives me my sense of belonging; God the Son gives me my worth in dying for me; and God the Holy Spirit makes me competent. But am I really worth anything if I'm not married? The third lie—feelings of incompleteness without a mate—destroys many women. The path to godliness is built on the solid conviction that a woman can be totally fulfilled, married or single.

God did surprise me with Jim. At the time, I was thoroughly satisfied with God's call to be single. I did not feel cheated. My self-worth did not depend on finding a husband. I wasn't even looking for one.

As a counselor to college students, I found the joy of God's fulfilled promises:

*F*ear the LORD, *you his saints,*
   for those who fear him lack nothing.
The lions may grow weak and hungry,
   but those who seek the LORD lack
no good thing.

Psalm 34:9-10

*D*elight *yourself in the* LORD
and he will give you the desires of
your heart.

Psalm 37:4

I didn't lack any good thing. God satisfied my heart's desires. As I traveled to about twenty Ohio campuses, helping students to grow in their walk with God and to share their faith, I had everything I needed.

God provided all this good, but he used many different people. They gave me a bed, meals, encouragement, a place to laugh and relax, friendship; they volunteered hours at conferences or on campus; and they contributed to my support. I learned to depend on God, and he was enough.

By this time, God had delivered me from husband hunting. I hated the image of a lioness on the prowl and vowed never to be one again. At one time I had tried to fill my God-shaped vacuum with a person or things, but satisfaction had eluded me. God was filling that emptiness as only he could. As a single woman, I could say, "I lack no good thing."

Singleness brought its own rewards and challenges. No longer did I depend on my parents or on college authorities. My ministry to students put me into situations where I was sometimes in over my head. My supervisor lived in another state. These tests taught me to lean on God alone.

Most important in my pursuit of godliness, Jesus himself became more personal to me. I often sang one of John Newton's hymns that expressed my response of praise for the direction of my life.

Then God yelled, "Surprise!" Just when I had proved that "those who seek the LORD lack no good thing," he brought Jim into my life. God taught me that some good gifts are mutually exclusive of other good gifts.

God wanted to give me the good gifts of a husband and children. Accepting them meant relinquishing some gifts that I presently enjoyed. The gift of marriage replaced the gift of singleness. The gift of children replaced the gift of freedom to travel from campus to campus discipling students.

Later, Jim told me that God had also spoken to him about finding fullness only in Jesus Christ, not in a spouse. God even used some of the same verses he had given to me. "For in Christ all the fullness of the Deity lives in bodily form, and *you have been given fullness in Christ,* who is the head over every power and authority" (Colossians 2:9-10, italics added).

Jim and I were two whole people, completely worthy to God, brought together by God as complements to each other. Jim and I work hard on complementing each other so that we cooperate, not compete, with each other. We want God to use us to build self-worth in each other.

Nor does having a husband remove a woman's need to depend on God alone. I often wonder how much time God spends creating new opportunities for me to depend on him. At first I marveled when appliances broke down and the children got sick when Jim was out of town. Anything that could go wrong seemed to go wrong when he wasn't around. God reminded me that my dependence was still on him, not on my husband.

God "has given us *everything we need for life and godliness* through our knowledge of him who called us by his own glory and goodness" (2 Peter 1:3, italics added). "Everything" includes our worth in God's sight, our competence in the Holy Spirit, and our wholeness in God alone, whether we are married or single. Because God has already given us all we need for physical and spiritual life out of his adequate and good provision, we can step confidently along the path to godliness with head held high.

Chapter Seven

Getting Along with the Hard-to-Get-Along-With

Along the way, gentleness

Three-hundred-pound tackle William "Refrigerator" Perry, a national football hero, appeared on TV proudly cuddling his three-pound premature daughter. One massive hand cradled the tiny infant. His enormous other paw—his ring size is twenty-three, the circumference of a half-dollar—tenderly stroked the baby's delicate fingers.

What is your mental image of gentleness? Unfortunately, gentleness gets bad press. For example, many people picture gentleness as a Mr. Milquetoast groveling at everyone's feet. Or they think of a woman allowing everyone in the office to walk over her in hobnail boots, ignoring her emotional screams and bruises.

But like Refrigerator Perry with his baby, gentleness does not equal weakness. Gentleness motivates the weary mother when her well-fed, dry baby refuses to sleep after hours and hours of rocking, walking, singing, and cuddling.

Jesus describes himself as "gentle and humble in heart" (Matthew 11:29). God assesses "a gentle and quiet spirit" (1 Peter 3:4) as having great value. So we can be sure that one discovery along the path to godliness will lead to gentleness. Before you decide to detour around that part of the path, let's see how gentleness looks, first in Jesus, and then in women today.

How is Jesus, the Lord of the universe, gentle? Recall some scenes from his life. He tenderly took children in his arms. Parents were so impressed by his gentleness that they brought their little ones to him. When a woman of the street crashed a dinner party in a religious man's house so that she could wash Jesus' feet with her tears, he defended her to his host and lovingly forgave her. With grieving sisters at their brother's grave, he wept, and then he called Lazarus back to life. Walking on the beach with Peter, Jesus forgave and restored him, even after Peter had turned his back on him.

But Jesus also called self-righteous men hypocrites, drove greedy money changers out of the temple with a whip, and rebuked frightened disciples for their lack of faith. Like a parent with trying children, Jesus dealt gently with irritating people. He did not rebuke them out of pompous pride and dominating selfishness like a petty tyrant; he rebuked them solely for their good.

For example, one day as Jesus was teaching in the temple, the take-charge Pharisees dragged in a woman caught in adultery (see John 8:3-11). Trembling, the terrified woman stood in front of them, the object of their glaring eyes and clicking tongues. These religious frauds hoped to trap Jesus into saying something that would be self-incriminating. Justice and mercy were not on their agenda for either Jesus or the woman.

Instead of answering them, or saying anything to the weeping woman awaiting execution, Jesus simply bent over and began to write in the dirt with his finger.

The frustrated Pharisees persisted in their questioning, but Jesus, in his own good time, coolly straightened up and shot the arrow at them: "If any one of you is without sin, let him be the first to throw a stone at her."

Calmly, quietly, perfectly self-controlled, he stooped down again and went on writing on the dirty temple floor. I wish I could have peered over his shoulder. Did he write the words *lies, greed, jealousy, false witness, murder, stealing, coveting?*

Whatever Jesus wrote, he emptied the temple. Conscience stricken, the accusers drifted away. He was soon left alone with the frightened, condemned woman, still standing before him, head bowed, like a lamb awaiting slaughter.

Jesus stood up and gently asked, "Woman, where are your accusers? Hasn't anyone condemned you?"

"No one, sir," she whispered anxiously, still not daring to lift her eyes.

"Then neither do I condemn you," Jesus assured her in a clear, firm voice. "Go now and leave your life of sin."

The temple sizzled with tension when Jesus confronted a roomful of sinners. But his strong gentleness accomplished two things: (1) the self-righteous faced the evil in their own hearts, and (2) the adulteress, who knew her sin, found forgiveness and a fresh start for her life.

61

How can we translate that kind of gentleness into our aggressive, me-first world? What does a gentle, quiet spirit look like in a woman today?

Stories from the Journey

Gentleness describes our pastor's wife. She often invited me to sit with her in church and always greeted me by name, and with a hug. I felt poor and ugly when I compared myself to beautiful Janelle and Anna with the nicest dresses. But when I sat with Mrs. M., felt her arm around me, and talked to her, I felt like the most special girl in the world.

Robin, 20s ■

Gentleness sprouts from the self-worth described in the last chapter. Knowing my supreme value in God's eyes and knowing that he makes me competent and whole, I don't have to go on the defensive when someone attacks me. Nor do I need to step on another person to make myself feel more important.

One of my professional acquaintances in Chicago, let's call her Virginia, epitomizes gentleness. Tall, neatly dressed, quiet, unassuming, and self-assured, she makes her office a comfortable and productive place to work. She sets a remarkable standard of excellence for herself and for her subordinates. Without waving a feminist flag, she has gained male respect by her careful, thorough work.

Virginia treats everyone respectfully. Everyone from the janitor on up talked about how much they missed her warm smile and her encouraging words when she was in the hospital.

Virginia's calm reduced the panic level in people. That's the power of gentleness. Under the pressure of finishing a major project, one of her co-workers was ready to explode. Instead of ignoring it or complaining about her irritability, Virginia asked warmly, "Is there anything we could do to help tame this monster?"

The young woman in the pressure cooker heard the gentleness, not criticism. She needed someone to notice the overwhelming size of her job and her mounting frustration.

When Virginia found out that one of her staff had a learning disability, she took time to encourage him. Without a tone of pity, she told him that she was impressed with his work. He had done well despite his disability. She asked him what things were hard for him and what things he could do easily. That's gentleness.

Gentleness is a prime ingredient in a happy marriage, especially when personalities get in the way. I often think about Ellen and Pete, who married young, very unsure of themselves.

Over the years, Ellen has learned her value in God's eyes, and now she is secure in his acceptance. But Pete remains immature, fearful, insecure. One failure after another on the job has reinforced his insecurity and driven him further into his shell. He pursues his hobbies as if he were single. He may go for days without speaking to Ellen. Such unhappiness with himself impels him to be defensive.

This volatile relationship could well erupt disastrously, except for one thing—Ellen's gentleness. "I've learned not to attack his walls, but to keep my sense of humor, talk about his good points, and wait out his silence without panic," Ellen confided, knowing that gentleness can wait patiently.

She could say this without a trace of self-pity but with a sparkle in her soft brown eyes. She gave me extremely wise counsel: "I know that I have to keep growing as a person, even if Pete doesn't. At first he felt threatened when I took classes or a part-time job to learn new things. But now he sees that these things have not taken me away from him. Instead, they've made me a more interesting person to live with."

Ellen is a realist, intensely practical. She takes risks; she is firm with her husband about her needs. They have seen other couples destroy each other in divorce. They know their marriage isn't perfect, but they say it's far better than divorce.

Stories from the Journey

 When one of my children screamed and howled, I would hold her on my lap and say firmly but softly, "I want you to cry quietly. It's all right to cry. But cry quietly."

Recently my daughter Linda told me how she hated that. "I wanted to scream. But now when I baby-sit, I say, 'I want you to cry quietly.'"

Rhoda, 50s, mother of five, grandmother of two ■

Jesus' style of gentleness helps us to live successfully with hard-to-get-along-with people. Plus, it brings its own rewards, like this one. One of my most cherished moments with Ellen brought her to me with all the bubbly excitement of a new bride. I could hardly contain myself until she told me what happened on their twenty-second anniversary. Pete had given her twenty-two long-stemmed red roses. "I'm reaping the benefits of investing twenty-two years in building a friendship," she said with all the anticipation of a mountain climber nearing the long-awaited summit.

In a professional assertiveness training seminar, you are taught to avoid being either passive or aggressive. For example, you shouldn't be a doormat, but neither should you attack another person. Learn to say what you feel and need. On the other hand, learn to listen to others and treat them as you would like to be treated.

Along the path to godliness, God requires a similar gentleness training seminar. Take the course from Jesus and become a gentle person.

Chapter Eight

Ever-Widening Concentric Circles

Along the way, prayer

My sister-in-law broke the news to me after my brother's surgery. Her voice choked as we talked on the phone. "The doctors say Sonny's liver cancer is inoperable and untreatable. They give him three to four months to live."

Stunned, I sat frozen to the spot. Just two months ago at our daughter Sara's wedding he seemed his usual jovial self. When the caterer kept blowing fuses in our kitchen during the reception, Sonny found the problem and rearranged the coffeepots on different circuits. He did look tired and his color didn't seem quite right, but liver cancer!

Helplessness gripped me. Questions flogged my mind. *How soon could we get to Louisville? What would we say or do when we got there?* For years we had prayed for my brother to make a Christian profession, but with no apparent results.

Mother's last prayer had been that her family would be with her in heaven, all of us.

Sonny was sixty-four. His single passion for success had taken him to the upper echelons of his company, but his keen interest in people, politics, and business drove him to over-work. He hated to fail at anything. And, by modern standards, he had achieved the American dream. Yet God was not a significant element in all that Sonny strove to do. He grew up seeing genuine Christianity in our family. He deeply loved and honored our parents, and he respected their faith. But they had both died without the assurance that Sonny had made any public commitment of his life to Christ.

Over the years, every time we saw each other, I prayed for some natural opening to discuss spiritual issues. But it never came. Now, as I hung up the phone, I doubted that I had the faith to ask for an opportunity to talk to Sonny about Jesus. But God reminded me of our church's prayer chain, so I called and asked for help.

Hanging on to that slim thread of hope, we left for Louis-ville. During the six-hour drive, I vacillated between asking for an opening and fearing that it would come. My faith dangled in the wind like a shattered branch. Fearfully, I spelled out the alternatives to Jim.

"What if we get there and don't get to talk to Sonny about Jesus? I don't think I could stand that. But if we open the conversation and Sonny isn't interested, I don't think I can stand that either."

The flat, dull, brown-and-gray Indiana cornfields stretched for miles along Interstate 65, capturing the essence of my mood. Obviously, I wasn't praying in faith. But I took courage from the man who said to Jesus, "I do believe; help me overcome my unbelief" (Mark 9:24). That honest confession, a mixture of faith and doubt, was enough for Jesus to heal the man's son. God's power does not depend on the size or perfection of my faith. A glimmer of hope rose on the horizon of my soul.

Not my strong faith but my helplessness pushed me to keep on praying. Helplessness produces healthy prayers. Years earlier, this theme had unveiled new riches in prayer for me. I had found it in O. Hallesby's classic *Prayer.*

Your helplessness is your best prayer. It calls from your heart to the heart of God with greater effect than all your uttered pleas. He hears it from the very moment that you are seized with helplessness, and he becomes actively engaged at once in hearing and answering the prayer of your helplessness.

Helplessness has now become the quiet, sustaining power of one's prayer life. A humble and contrite heart knows that it can merit nothing before God, and that all that is necessary is to be reconciled to one's helplessness and let our holy and almighty God care for us, just as an infant surrenders himself to his mother's care.

Mother and Daddy had prayed desperately out of helplessness. They could not change their son; they could only pray and wait. But in those long years of silence, God had been listening.

Sonny did come to faith in Christ. God opened the door I had been praying for, even with my mustard seed of faith.

All day Saturday, visitors, doctors, and nurses streamed in and out of Sonny's hospital room. Private conversation was impossible. As we trudged down the hall to the elevators, my heart felt like a huge boulder in my chest.

Hope almost flickered out, but I said to myself and to God, "Surely Sunday morning we can talk if Jim and I sit with Sonny while the rest of the family go to church."

That's what we did. After what seemed like a year of casual conversation, we asked something that triggered Sonny's quick response. Weak, but coherent, in slow, carefully measured words, he said: "I want to be forgiven. I'm not the man I ought to be. Every day I ask for forgiveness. Anyone who had parents like we had knows they are in heaven. I want to be with them. I need to be forgiven."

God had been speaking to him all those years, although we had seen no evidence of it. In wide-eyed astonishment, I listened to what Sonny had been thinking and wishing about his life. He poured out his regrets, his misunderstandings, and now his eagerness to accept God's forgiveness. Strength surged into his cancer-ridden body. Clearly, he thanked Jesus for dying for him.

Crying, hugging, and laughing, we basked in the heat of God's grace. Time rocketed past. Suddenly, we had to leave. After a final hug, Sonny gripped my hand. With his voice and his eyes he told me, "I believe everything we said. I know it's all true."

I did not know that those would be the last words I would ever hear my brother say. But I clasp them in my heart as part of God's most precious treasures to me. God mercifully set Sonny free in less than three months.

Cancer focused Sonny's full attention on God. In mercy, God halted him in his hectic world, and he listened. God honored all those years of our prayers of helplessness and faithfully kept his promises.

Stories from the Journey

 Several years ago, I attended a retreat where we were asked to write positive characteristics of the person next to us.

When my smiling neighbor handed me what she had written about me, I was surprised. It said, "A prayer warrior." That was certainly not a title I'd give myself. But that's what the slip of paper said. And my smiling neighbor was right.

At times I feel an urgency to pray for someone, especially in the middle of the night. I awake often because one of my children is coughing or crying out. Instead of fuming over my plight, I begin to pray for others.

News of answers to some of my prayers encourages me to trust God for those I may never hear about.

My prayers have changed over the years from, "Please do this, or heal that," to "Please give spiritual insight and endurance, build character, manifest the fruit of the Spirit in these lives." I hope to become like the prayer warrior described in Ephesians 6:18:

"Pray in the spirit on all occasions with all kinds of prayers and requests. With this in mind, be alert and always keep on praying for all the saints."

Sandy, 40s, mother of two ■

A story from Israel's history impresses me with the necessity of praying for my family, especially my nieces and nephews. When Judah's King Ahaziah was killed, his wicked mother, Athaliah, attempted to destroy the whole royal family so that she could reign without a rival (2 Chronicles 22:10-12). She would have succeeded, except for the quick action of Jehosheba, her stepdaughter. Jehosheba stole into the palace nursery and rescued baby Joash, her nephew. She and her husband hid and protected Joash for six years until the time was right for him to be declared the rightful king. God used a godly aunt to fulfill his purpose for her nephew.

In one of our Sunday school classes, we got to know Polly. She is the godly aunt in this case. Her niece, Donna, rejects all of her family's values and suffers from the consequences of drug abuse, divorce, and unemployment. Consistently, she rebuffs her aunt, but Polly continues to pray, love, and be kind. Recently, Donna, in desperation and with no place to go, asked another aunt if she could move in with her.

Now she attends church with the family and has begun to see a Christian counselor. God's creativity and sense of humor shine through such "coincidences." The counselor is the daughter of Donna's mother's best friend. The people whose values she rejects are those whom God is now using to heal her. Meanwhile, Polly keeps watching and praying like a modern-day Jehosheba.

But God's concern is bigger than just our families. He requires "that requests, prayers, intercession and thanksgiving be made for everyone" (1 Timothy 2:1).

For those of us who grew up in homes in which we were prayed for before we were born, it's hard to believe that there are some adults who have never known that anyone would pray for them. In a neighborhood Bible study group, I met Louise, and that was her story.

It all started in Brenda's car en route to our study. As Louise got into the car, she threw down her cigarette in disgust.

"I wish I could kick this dreadful habit," she moaned.

Without hesitation, Brenda said, "I'll pray for you to be able to stop."

As soon as they arrived, Louise burst into the living room and announced, "Do you know what Brenda just said to me? She said she would pray for me! I've never known anyone who prayed for me in my whole life."

Imagine how isolated and alone Louise must have felt, never knowing that anyone cared enough to pray for her. Her story moves me to pray for others along the path to godliness, as well as for those who haven't found the path yet.

For my prayer vision, I like to picture ever-widening concentric circles: myself, my family, and my friends; my neighbors, my church; the church around the world, missionaries; those in prison for their faith; rulers at every level of government; judges and justices; the poor and oppressed; and so on.

Stories from the Journey

 My husband and I enrolled in language school in Jordan to learn Arabic. We managed to cope with all the stresses of cross-cultural living. But I felt the creative, artistic part of me was dying. I loved all kinds of needlework, crafts, creating designs. I kept praying, "Lord, can't you use these gifts you've given me? For years you've given me opportunities to use other talents. What about this part of me?" Then one day I met a neighbor, Nihad, head of a development project teaching poor women to embroider. The refugees and other poor women desperately needed work they could do in their homes to help feed their families. For five years Nihad had been praying for someone to help who knew color and design and had an eye for what would sell to foreigners.

We laughed, cried, and praised God as we realized *he* had brought us together as the answer to each other's prayers.

Beverly, 30s, mother of two ∎

I happen to be a list maker. So, a daily prayer list with names from each circle galvanizes my good intentions into action. If I don't know someone's immediate struggles, I like to use a prayer from the Bible for that individual. For young friends making decisions and setting the course of their lives, I often pray:

We constantly pray for you, that our God may count you worthy of his calling, and that by his power he may fulfill every good purpose of yours and every act prompted by your faith. We pray this so that the name of our Lord Jesus may be glorified in you, and you in him, according to the grace of our God and the Lord Jesus Christ

2 Thessalonians 1:11-12

What more can I ask than that their good purposes and acts of faith would be empowered by God? Or that Jesus would be glorified in them? God's grace makes this possible. This prayer represents God's perspective on their real needs, which is far superior to my requests for their health and safety.

One young friend in whom God has been answering this prayer grew up in the church Jim pastored. Following is her story.

Stories from the Journey

 When I was in junior high, I dreamed of being an archaeologist and avidly devoured books on the subject. For years, my parents took my sister and I with them one night a week to lead the program in the church's youth center. Games, crafts, Bible study, conversations over homemade cupcakes created a loving, fun, safe evening for children who had little exposure to the church. My parents' example kindled my desire to serve Jesus by investing myself in the lives of young people who need to know him. During college, I learned the realities of inner city living.

Archaeology gave way to a desire to work with inner-city youth, and I moved into West Philadelphia, as part of a team creating ministries to meet the social, educational, and spiritual needs of the children and young people.

God has been teaching me a major prayer lesson. Instead of asking God to bless our plans, we need to ask God what plans we should make. We came up with wonderful ministry ideas. We asked God to bless these plans and spent time and energy carrying out each new idea only to see it either fail or fade away after the energy and enthusiasm wore off. Discouraged, we concluded that God wasn't doing anything here. In April 1991 the need for some type of community worship experience for young people discouraged by traditional church services gripped me. I immediately began to plan: who to invite, order of worship, building, etc. But some inner warning said, *Wait. Well, Lord, why give me such a strong desire and then make me wait? It will never happen that way,* I thought. But I did wait, occasionally reminding God of the idea he had given me.

Still the answer came, *Wait.* In May '92, one of the local young men, who grew up with drugs, gangs, etc. but now demonstrated the change Jesus had made in his life, came to me with an idea. The community needed a youth church for teens turned off by traditional services. He had a building

available, a target group—the kids we worked with all the
school year—and a time and date, July 19 at 6:00 P.M.

If I had pushed the idea last year, I would have been working alone, had to find the building, and beg the kids to come.
Instead, God brought a local person with the same desire, a
building, and a target group ready for the experience! WOW!
The name of Jesus is being glorified in me in ways I could
not have imagined or known to ask.

Judy, 30s ■

During my daily Bible reading, God often supplies a verse
or an idea to form a prayer for those for whom I'm interced-
ing. Reading the newspaper and news magazines motivates
me to pray and informs my prayer life. As I write this book,
South Africa and the former Yugoslavia are in crises. So I
pray for the rulers and the churches in those countries. May
the rulers listen to wise counsel and act for justice rather than
political advantage. May the Christians' faith be unshaken;
may they be comforted by God; may they be as harmless as
doves and as wise as serpents; may they use opportunities to
tell of God's peace and grace.

Not all of our prayers produce the results we want. Even
after years of waiting, the answer to a legitimate request may
be no. God is not our errand boy. He can't be manipulated by
our formulas, bargains, or tears. This was a traumatic lesson
for me to learn. Many of you can identify with me in this
painful experience.

To have a baby is a normal, reasonable request for a couple
to make. Jim and I happily anticipated having a baby to
complete our family with Sara and John. In our family prayers

we began to ask, "Lord, please give us a baby brother or sister for Sara and John."

One day at the amusement park, we came to the wishing well, and Sara confidently threw in her penny and wished, "I want a baby sister."

But months of hoping, praying, and wishing turned into years of futility. Every month my emotions rose and fell along with my daily temperature readings. Disappointment mounted. We had reserved our back bedroom for a nursery, but eventually we gave it to a Korean student who wanted to live with us to improve her English.

The final blow came when the doctor spoke to me across his desk very matter-of-factly. "I'll be glad to sign any papers for an adoption application. I can state that you and your husband have completed all the medical avenues open to you." It was as if he stabbed me, twisted the knife, and didn't even notice. I still cringe when I recall that awful day.

Somehow I managed to get home, barely able to see where I was driving, at times disoriented, not even sure if I was on the right street. Sorrow and anger alternately rained blows on me like a jackhammer. How could the doctor slam the door shut in my face? How could he tell me to stop hoping? My Bible bore dates scribbled next to the promises that I had claimed over the months as we had prayed for a baby.

I believe that I shall see the goodness of the LORD in the land of the living! Wait for the LORD; be strong,

> and let your heart take courage;
> *yea, wait for the LORD!*

Psalm 27:13-14, RSV

Surely a baby was part of the goodness of the Lord! We had waited on the Lord. My heart had taken courage again and again, but my good request was being refused without any explanation.

Thanksgiving Day approached. The thought of going to church paralyzed me because people stood and thanked God for specific blessings of the year. Resentment boiled over. I did not want to hear other people tell me how good God was to them when he was saying no to me.

I rationalized an airtight case against God. How could I thank him for turning a deaf ear to my cries for something that he said was good! God owed me an answer. Besides, how could I sit there weeping in my disappointment? I certainly could not smile and pretend that everything was fine.

But then one of those parts of the Bible that I had stored away crashed into my consciousness. The ageless question that God had addressed to Job pinned me to the wall: "Will the one who contends with the Almighty correct him? Let him who accuses God answer him!" (Job 40:2).

My choices suddenly illuminated my mind like the headlights of a car peering down a dark, deserted country lane. I could curse this God who didn't give me the good thing I wanted, or I could worship him for who he is. Those were my alternatives.

Stories from the Journey

 Someone said God has four answers to prayer:
1. Yes, I thought you'd never ask.
2. Yes, and here's more.
3. No, not now.
4. No, I love you too much.

Joann, 40s, mother of two ∎

Is God wise, good, merciful, powerful, loving, faithful, and gracious? If so, then he can be trusted with a no. He doesn't owe me an explanation. Faith is being certain of what I do not see. If I could see why God was saying no to my request, I would be living by sight, not by faith.

If I worship God only because he gives me what I want, I insult him. If a child loves a parent only to get gifts, he isn't honoring the parent. The parent's wisdom and love can be trusted. I must worship God for himself alone. I must focus on the wise and loving Giver, not on a gift.

God tenderly nourished me back to health. His patience is inexhaustible. My anger, fear, and disappointment subsided. Calmness flowed over my soul like a soothing balm of a warm bath.

I don't remember what I said that Thanksgiving Day, but I do remember the choice I made not to curse my God when he says no, but to worship him instead. God's no to me was infinitesimally small compared with his no to Jesus in

Gethsemane when he agonized in prayer for some way to avoid the cross. God's no was part of his gracious work of conforming me to Jesus' image. It was a significant milestone on the path to godliness.

Chapter Nine

"Help Me Think Bigger!"

Along the way, worship

O ne night at church, a young man who had just returned from three years in Beirut, Lebanon, jolted my idea of worship. He said, "When I went to Lebanon, I thought I knew who God was. He was someone who wanted everyone to have a good day. But Lebanon changed my view. Now I see God as the only unshakable in a very shaky world."

War, terrorism, migraines, ulcers, friends blown apart by bombs convinced him that everything is temporary. He had no props to lean on. Everything was unstable.

The young man continued, "I also learned that God sees in the dark while we blindly grope along, afraid of stumbling. He trains the blind to depend on him, even when the blind are his own servants.

" 'Who is blind but my servant, and deaf like the messenger I send? Who is blind like the one committed to me, blind like the servant of the LORD?' (Isaiah 42:19).

83

"But God promises to lead the blind along unfamiliar paths. 'I will lead the blind by ways they have not known, along unfamiliar paths I will guide them. I will turn the darkness into light before them and make the rough places smooth' (Isaiah 42:16). It's as though God moves the furniture in our dark house and then leads us safely across the room," he concluded.

Here were dramatic, new pictures of God: the only unshakable, the one who moves the furniture but leads us safely through the house.

"Lord, help me think bigger!" I cried. "I often worship you for all you give me. Help me worship you for who you are."

The Bible pictures God as my Father but also my Judge; my Shepherd but also my King; my Friend but also my Master. The prayers and visions of Moses, Job, David, Daniel, Isaiah, Jeremiah, John, Paul, and others in the Bible enlarge my ideas about God, like a telescope revealing the rings around Saturn.

Psalm 145 is a gold mine of ideas about God. The writer worships God for

- greatness
- the glorious splendor of his majesty
- power
- abundant goodness
- righteousness
- graciousness
- compassion
- slowness to anger and richness in love
- the glorious splendor of his kingdom
- everlasting endurance through all generations

- faithfulness to all his promises
- nearness to all who call on him
- holiness

Notice that the psalmist focuses on the kind of person God is, not on what he gives. To do that, I try to picture what those qualities of God look like. Greatness and goodness took shape for me when Eva Mills, a retired English missionary, told me her story.

Eva was engaged to a missionary veterinarian working in the Amazon River valley. In 1928, she hoped to go from England to Brazil to join him, but her father opposed her going to such a primitive place. After months of praying and preparing, she finally received her father's approval. To prove his change of heart, he made a chest to carry her equipment.

She told me, "Father spent his evenings at his workshop in the basement, working on that project for me. It was a mahogany chest, his own idea, just a loving proof of his willingness to stand by me. The chest was of half-inch mahogany, and the lid was of one piece, about eighteen inches wide and thirty inches long. Not a nail did he use; the chest was all dovetailed together and made secure with a brass lock. It was definitely made for endurance. . . .

"Because the mahogany chest proved too small to carry all my collection of needed articles, Father emptied his own tool chest, one he had made when a boy of fourteen. It was the same size as the new, beautifully polished mahogany chest, already full."

The day Eva arrived in Brazil, she and David were married in a civil ceremony and in a Christian ceremony, all in Portuguese. After a few days of living in one room behind a vegetable shop, they boarded a riverboat for an eight-day journey upriver. At a riverside town, they began their trek over a mountain to reach the village in which they would live. All their belongings had to be carried on mule back over the mountain trails.

The men loaded the mule with one of her wooden chests on each side. They smiled and pointed to the perfectly balanced load. The chests were the maximum size that a mule could carry over the mountain trail.

What greatness and goodness! God knew what Eva and David would need in the Amazon jungle in 1928. So a generation before a fourteen-year-old boy had built a tool chest, and as an adult, he had built a matching one for his daughter, not knowing what plans God had for them.

Graciousness was illustrated for me in the life of Olga, a graduate student from Austria. She had majored in physical education and English literature at an Austrian university. Attractive and popular, she was a good student and an excellent athlete, but she was also anti-Christian.

I have no reason to be a Christian. I have everything I need—friends, health, good grades. Christianity is for people who need a crutch, she thought.

In her skiing classes, Olga noticed two interesting fellows who were different from the other students. In spite of the fierce competition among the athletes, they didn't make winning their number one goal. On the ski slopes if some of the girls fell behind, they would slow down and allow the girls to catch up with them.

Near the end of the term, Olga was trying to finish a paper and type it before an impending deadline.

"I'll never get this paper typed on time. My hunt-and-peck method takes forever," she moaned one day after class.

"Could John and I type it for you?" Hans asked.

Olga had never heard of any student offering to type a paper for another student. She couldn't figure out what made John and Hans help her, but she was grateful.

When the fellows had invited her to a Bible study, she had told them she wasn't interested. But after they helped her with her term paper, she decided she should go once just to see what a Christian meeting was like. She was in for more surprises. The people at the meeting weren't social and academic misfits huddled together for support. They were attractive students talking about Jesus Christ as though he were someone they knew. Her curiosity about these Christians kept her talking and asking questions.

When Olga decided to teach German in England for a year, Hans and John gave her a Bible to take along. She had chosen the town in which to teach from a postcard. It pictured a marvelous English seaside town with crowded beaches and happy vacationers. What a great place to teach German while she improved her English! But no one had told her that the same seaside town was a sleepy, cold, gray village in the winter.

Olga arrived in the village in late summer after the crowds had disappeared. She couldn't imagine how the post card picture could really be of this beach. The children taking German were scattered throughout the town, so she had to take buses to the various schools. That meant she didn't have a classroom of her own or an opportunity to be part of one faculty. The other teachers ignored her cries for help or friendship.

One day she realized that she wasn't the girl who had everything. She had no friends, no skiing, no recognition. The whole world was gray and turning black. Of all the places in the world she could have gone to teach, she came to this village. Since there was no one else to turn to, she decided to turn to God. She dug out the Bible Hans and John had given her and began to read.

At mid-year she resigned her job and returned to the university in Austria. "I thought I had everything in the world I needed. But God took me to a place where I had nothing. Stripped of what I thought was important, I realized I need God," she told Hans and John.

In graciousness, God brought Olga to himself. He gave her opportunities to learn about him and about her need. He waited patiently for her to discover the truth about herself. He put her in the right place so that she could make those discoveries.

Stories from the Journey

 What stimulates me to worship? The sunrise in my rearview mirror while driving to work ("When Morning Gilds the Skies"); great sacred choral works sung at our new Presbyterian church; the black gospel music led by the Union Tabernacle Church of God in Christ at our monthly joint worship. Hymns and classical music tend to show me the greatness of God ("Joyful, Joyful We Adore Thee"); while gospel songs ("Jesus, What a Friend of Sinners") help me experience his tenderness. Black gospel songs make me feel hopeful in God's goodness and lift my spirits remarkably. Praise choruses help me memorize Scripture and focus on a single theme.

Worship leaves me feeling filled up so I have energy to respond to needs of other people. It can remind me of things I need to make right with another person. In worship I lose my fear of facing God honestly, even about being angry with him. Many times when I feel disconnected from God, I'm really disconnected from myself. But as soon as I allow myself to face the pain I instinctively bury, God is there!

Worship restores my sense of balance. I go to church because I need to be with a group of people that affirms that there is more to this world than what we see. The "make it happen" pressure on my job, as a commissioned salesperson, assumes that we create our destiny. God's sovereignty is the weight I need to balance the scale.

Carol Joy, 30s ■

On a brisk September day as I was hiking near the Garden of the Gods in Colorado, I got the feeling of the glorious splendor of his majesty. The sky was that unbelievable Colorado blue. A flock of mountain chickadees flitted through the trees. A deer grazed nearby. Three bighorn mountain sheep picked their way across a step slope. Wind-sculptured red rocks rose hundreds of feet in the air. Snow-crowned Pikes Peak reflected the sun. The red giants were silhouetted against the blue sky or against Pikes Peak if I turned.

What I saw and heard made me want to worship God. I sang all the hymns of praise I knew and tried to think of a psalm about creation but couldn't. When I returned to the motel, I found Psalm 148 and began to memorize it.

Praise the LORD.

Praise the LORD from the heavens,
praise him in the heights above.
Praise him, all his angels,
praise him, all his heavenly hosts.
Praise him, sun and moon,
praise him, all you shining stars.
Praise him, you highest heavens
and you waters above the skies.
Let them praise the name of
the LORD.
for he commanded and they
were created.
He set them in place for ever
and ever;
he gave a decree that will never
pass away.

Praise the LORD from the earth,
you great sea creatures and
all ocean depths,
lightning and hail, snow and clouds,

stormy winds that do his bidding,
you mountains and all hills,
fruit trees and all cedars,
wild animals and all cattle,
small creatures and flying birds,
kings of the earth and all nations,
you princes and all rulers
on earth,
young men and maidens,
old men and children.

Let them praise the name of
the LORD,
for his name alone is exalted;
his splendor is above the earth
and the heavens,
He has raised up for his people
a horn,
the praise of all his saints,
of Israel, the people close to
his heart.

Praise the LORD.

The psalmist and I both looked at our world and learned our true size. Worship gives me a proper perspective on my own importance. I appreciate how Phillips Brooks expresses the idea: "The true way to be humble is not to stoop until you are smaller than yourself, but to stand at your real height against some higher nature that will show you what the real smallness of your greatness is."

Stories from the Journey

My daily worship often begins with a song in my mind when I awaken. Who but the Holy Spirit could plant a hymn perfectly suited to my needs that day? The cabinet drawer next to my favorite chair holds my Bible, my prayer notebook, and a hymnal.

I love to read a psalm and pray it back to God. The psalmist's description of God and his works becomes my worship expression.

Some psalms have more ideas about God than I can pray through and apply in one day.

Worship really goes on all day. As I walk, I pray, "Thank you Lord, for that brilliant yellow maple tree and for the Lord Jesus, fairer than all the forest." At work as I change addresses in the computer, I pray, "Heavenly Father, comfort this person who has moved. The adjustments may be hard and lonely."

Next to the Bible, the hymnal is my most treasured book. In the last three months since my husband, Paul's death, I've kept a copy of the hymn I chose for his memorial service in front of me. On the kitchen counter, on the dresser, "It Is Well with My Soul" expresses my praise and prayer to God.

A verse from "Children of the Heavenly Father" has become my song in the night.

"Though he giveth or he taketh,
God his children ne'er forsaketh;
His the loving purpose solely
To preserve them pure and holy."

Betty, 80s, mother of four, grandmother of eleven,
great-grandmother of ten ■

Worship is a public as well as a personal experience along the path to godliness. I love singing God's praises with the whole congregation, standing shoulder to shoulder and focusing attention on him, listening to others sing about God, sitting silently in his presence, meditating on his character.

In both public and private worship, I appreciate a minimum of distractions, uncluttered space, silence, word pictures of God, unhurried time, and music. In such a setting, I regain a proper perspective on my own size and on God.

I hope you find such a place to worship, whether it's in a small circle of students in a college classroom, in a one-room church, in an inner-city church, in a large suburban church, in a park at sunrise on Easter, or in a colosseum. It isn't the size of the building and congregation that matters but our being a part of "a royal priesthood, a holy nation, a people belonging to God," declaring the praises of God who called us "out of darkness into his wonderful light" (1 Peter 2:9).

Chapter Ten

Free to Say No, Free to Say Yes

Along the way, time

I plan my day carefully to pack in as much as possible. My dentist appointment is at 3:45. I know it takes only eight to ten minutes to get there. So at 3:35 I dash out the garage door. Oh, no! The school at the end of the block is just letting out. Cars line the street in both directions. Parents are picking up their children. I watch the minutes blink by on the digital dashboard clock.

Finally, I escape the school traffic, speed through the side streets, and reach the railroad crossing. A freight train, a long freight train! The clock keeps on blinking as I tap out the seconds on the steering wheel. When I finally open the door of the dentist's office, the clock behind the receptionist reads 3:50.

"We just took another patient. Your appointment was at 3:45," she says curtly.

"I know. There was a freight train," I reply as uneasily as a defendant before a judge.

"That'll do it." She smiles.

It didn't matter that last week I waited fifteen minutes for the dentist because he was late returning from lunch. No, I can wait until he finishes with the patient who took my place because I was five minutes late. Murphy's Law, "If something can go wrong, it will," has worked again.

Because getting control of my time has not been easy, I decided to try to figure out how Jesus, God in the flesh, controlled his time. I thought, *Since God is trying to make me like the Lord Jesus, perhaps I can learn something from his example.* I began reading the Gospel of Mark looking for clues.

The first clue I found was in the description of Jesus' refusal to do what his friends wanted him to do (see Mark 1:21-39). On the Sabbath, Jesus cast a demon out of a man in the synagogue, healed Peter's mother-in-law, and, after sunset, healed the sick and demon-possessed that the town of Capernaum brought to him. Before dawn the next morning, Jesus went out to pray in a lonely place.

When Peter and the other disciples found him, they complained, "Everyone is looking for you!"

Jesus surprised them by replying, "Let's go somewhere else. I'm not going back to Capernaum but on to other towns to preach there. That's what I came to do."

His friends were asking him to do a good thing, "Go back and heal more people as you did yesterday."

"They need you. You can do a lot of good here."

"I'm proud of you and proud to be your disciple."

They exerted heavy social pressure on Jesus. And so our friends do on us. *If we do what people expect, they'll like us and accept us,* we think. *At least we should do what our friends ask.*

But Jesus had a higher priority; preaching was more important than healing; and preaching in the whole country was more important than returning to Capernaum. Perhaps the pressure to please people and accept their agenda for him drove him out to pray before dawn. It should certainly drive us to pray about how to use our time. Knowing that preaching was his top priority enabled Jesus to say no to his friends' good request. Before God we must decide what comes first.

I found Jesus' second priority to serve people—when he told his disciples why he came, "For even the Son of Man did not come to be served, but to serve, and to give his life as a ransom for many" (Mark 10:45).

Jesus served people constantly, the poor, the tax collectors, the street women, the children, the blind beggars, the demon-possessed, Gentiles, crowds who robbed him of sleep and of time to eat.

Since serving people was his high priority, he could ignore social and economic standing, people's criticisms, his own convenience and comfort, and the religious traditions that had been added to God's laws by the legalists. How much of your time do these things take?

Supremely, Jesus came to die for the sins of others. In the crisis of betrayal, arrest, trial, and execution, he gave low priority to using his power to protect himself or to vindicate himself from false accusations.

Jesus set his top priorities: to preach, to serve, and to die. He responded to demands on his time and energy in light of those priorities.

Once he tried to take a day off with his weary disciples, but when they got to the vacation spot and saw five thousand people waiting for them, Jesus replaced Plan A with Plan B (see Mark 6:30-44). Instead of taking a day off, he taught the people and had the disciples feed them supper and clean up the crumbs. He didn't treat the crowd as an interruption, but as a group of people to be served.

However, after that day, Jesus kept looking for a time and place to get back to Plan A: time alone with his disciples. They had to travel farther and farther away to get the day off.

Jesus' example accents our need to set clear priorities. We can plan our time in light of those priorities, but we must be flexible to move to Plan B or Plan C if God gives us an opportunity to serve someone. Serving may or may not be convenient. But we don't give up on Plan A; we just reschedule it.

Does this really work? Let me give you an example of how it does. One January when I had set my priorities for the week, my schedule included after-Christmas cleaning, Bible studies, two committee meetings, correspondence, and so on. That was before I called my neighbor Pauline.

"You didn't hear what happened to me on Christmas Eve, did you?" she asked. "I fell on the ice and broke my arm. It'll be in a cast for a month."

"How terrible! Is there anything I can do to help? Do you need something from the store?" I responded in a burst of sympathy and helpfulness. Since I was going shopping that day, it would be easy to do her shopping. "No, my husband likes to shop, so I don't need anything from the store. One neighbor brought soup last night, and George can heat it again tonight. But getting dressed is one of my biggest problems, with the cast on my arm," she added plaintively.

I began to think of all the things I do in a day that I couldn't do with only one hand. Instead of thinking how I could help with the least amount of inconvenience to me, I began to think about what Pauline needed.

During the next month, that included helping Pauline dress, taking in meals, cleaning the bathroom and kitchen, washing her back, doing the laundry, and taking her to the beauty shop and to the doctor. Somehow God multiplied my time and energy in serving Pauline and George. And all my work at home that needed to be done got done.

Some of my priorities, such as loving and obeying God, will last my whole life. Other priorities have changed in different stages of my life. When I was a student, learning as much as I could learn and being a witness on campus were two priorities. When I was a teacher, teaching the class to think was my high priority. When I was an InterVarsity staff worker, helping students to mature in Christ was a top priority. When I was a mother of small children, introducing them to nature and to books were two priorities.

Jesus controlled his time, first, by setting his priorities and, second, by knowing who he was. At his baptism, the Father's voice announced to the crowd what Jesus had always known, "You are my Son, whom I love; with you I am well pleased" (Mark 1:11). Jesus could speak and act with freedom because his identity and value didn't depend on people's opinions of him or their treatment of him. He knew who he was in the Father's eyes.

Being confident that God has already accepted me as I am, and that he is the one to whom I must answer for use of my time and abilities, frees me to say no or yes to people's requests. I've learned to seldom give an answer on the phone to a request to serve on a committee or to take on a new responsibility. I ask what it will involve and promise to call back the next day to give my answer. That frees me from the pressure of high-powered sales talk, from saying yes to feed my ego or to please the person. Then I look at my schedule and ask God if this job is for me or someone else. Is there something I should drop to do this? If so, what can I drop?

Not being able to say no because of having to please everyone is one of the worst traps to be in. Florence is one of many people I've known in this trap. She grew up never being able to please her parents. If her report card had four A's and two Bs, they asked why she didn't have all A's. When she sang in the spring musical, her father pointed out the one time she was late on her entrance but said nothing about the rest of her performance.

At church she tried to live up to every expectation of the youth leaders. She had to be at every meeting, read the Bible more than anyone else in the group, have a longer prayer list, and keep every rule.

Now on her job, she works overtime, skips lunch, goes in on Saturdays, and attends night classes while she tries to participate in everything in the church and make frequent visits to see her family.

Florence tells me that she recognizes her pattern of letting people use her, of being a doormat. She doesn't get enough sleep and hardly ever takes time just for fun. She feels responsible to do everything she thinks people and God expect of her.

Intellectually, Florence knows that only by God's grace is she forgiven and accepted by him. But she struggles to live by grace rather than by her achievements. So she is enslaved to every demand for her time. She must do everything perfectly, and there is *never* enough time to do something perfectly.

Florence is a candidate for the new organization Superwomen Anonymous. Their motto is "Enough Is Enough." The founder, Carol Orsborn, formerly worked fifty hours a week as president of a large public relations agency. Since she cut her hours to thirty and moved to a scaled-down house that has "half of everything," she spends more time relaxing and getting to know her two children.

Her newsletter explores guilt-free unpopularity, the freedom to say no with a clear conscience. The amazing volume and quality of responses represents a huge, collective sigh of relief. Superwomen Anonymous has discovered that being martyrs or perfectionists doesn't help them or the people they serve.

Some readers of this book will not understand how anyone can act like Florence. Other readers will identify with her and cry for her. To those I want to recommend the book *Healing for Damaged Emotions* by David Seamands. From years as a pastor and counselor, Dr. Seamands has been able to help many Florences.

Let me introduce you to Betsy, a recovering Florence. For years she was controlled by the old tapes playing in her head. *You don't measure up. You aren't good enough to please people, and certainly not good enough to please God. Try harder. Try harder!*

Her low self-image drove her to severe depression, followed by years of counseling and slow healing. But today she is one of the freest women I know. When the old lies come back to mind, she practices what Paul recommends in Philippians 4:8. She thinks about what is *true*. She refuses to think about her being a worthless failure. Instead she thinks about Jesus counting her worth dying for, about God's accepting her as she is, and about God's gracious forgiveness as he makes her more like Jesus. With these new tapes playing in her head, she looks people in the eye with shoulders back and a welcoming smile, radiating confidence.

As I follow Jesus' examples in setting priorities and seeing myself from God's point of view, I begin to get control of my time. But I keep running into time robbers. These enemies of time control take many forms: oversleeping, procrastination, paper shuffling, "telephonitis," and so on. One of the most common time robbers is television.

When Jim was a pastor, several families in the congregation talked about their struggle to have time for family devotions or a fun night or just time to talk as a family. The television always seemed to interfere.

Several helpful ideas came out of our brainstorming for solutions. At the beginning of the week, the family looked over the TV schedule to choose programs they really wanted to see. The number of hours of TV viewing on school nights and on the weekend were set. Within those limits, the children could choose programs. The TV was turned on only when one of the preselected programs came on.

Another family started a Saturday morning tradition of eating breakfast at a pancake house. Everyone loved the menu. They talked about what happened that week. It's amazing how much more children talk to parents in restaurants than in the kitchen. No phone calls or visitors interrupted them. When they returned home, they could start a family project such as raking leaves, washing the car, or cleaning their rooms without dragging someone away from Saturday morning cartoons.

Another family decided to buy a VCR to record the weeknight programs that were worth seeing but interfered with doing homework or attending church. Then when the family was ready to watch television, there was something available.

Another family used the VCR to record the programs suitable for their preschooler. When he asked to watch TV, they weren't at the mercy of what the networks were showing at the moment.

Another family decided to sell their TV because it was controlling them. They wanted to read more, talk to each other, and be involved with a couples' Bible study, but they couldn't find a night away from some favorite TV program. They were addicted, so total abstinence was the answer for them at that point.

We've seen that controlling time involves (1) setting priorities, (2) being free to say no to time requests, (3) dealing with time robbers, and now (4) keeping a schedule. I have an appointment calendar at each phone for quick reference. At a glance I see my regular responsibilities and time blocked out for what is important to me, Bible study and worship, time with my family, time to relax, and time to build memories.

In trying to make my schedule consistent with what I believe is important, it sometimes gets too full. When that happens efficiency drops, fatigue sets in, and angry words are likely to erupt because I'm like a rubber band being stretched and stretched and not allowed to be relaxed. No wonder God set aside one day in seven for rest (see Exodus 20:8-11). A day off and vacations deserve priority status. But in between

I've learned to give myself a ten-minute vacation during the day. It may be a walk outside to listen to the birds, enjoy the flowers, and breathe deeply, or it may be a relaxation exercise on the floor.

Working in the flower garden provides great relaxation for me. Kneeling to dig, pull weeds, or transplant seedlings rests my mind and body. The variety of color, design, and textures in the flowers prompts me to praise God. Knowing that exercise reduces stress and makes us feel better, Jim and I make time to walk two miles a day around the neighborhood.

After the top priorities are scheduled, I can choose to give my time to the people and jobs I wish. When I choose to give time rather than doing it as a people pleaser, I enjoy it more and so do others.

Stories from the Journey

 Sometimes I want to do more for God, but I feel hindered by where I am now—mother of four and wife of a pastor. I need the reminder that different priorities go with different times in our lives. I get consumed by what people will think of me if I don't do more, or that life will pass me by if I don't do more. What a great encouragement that my loving heavenly Father just wants me to trust and love him more than anything.

Yvonne, 40s, mother of four ■

Working mothers must have the hardest job of anyone making schedules match priorities. For some women, working isn't a choice. If they don't work, their children don't eat or have a home. Those women need all the encouragement and help the church and society can give. They fight the battle of false guilt for not being at home with their children.

But many women do have a choice of working full-time or part-time or of being at home with their children. The bonding process between parent and child takes longer than the usual maternity leave. Studies indicate that a child's basic character is formed in the first three years. That critical period in a child's life needs all the attention *parents* can give. Those can be the hardest years in parenting, but they aren't intellectual suicide.

Sandy, a young mother, wrote to tell me she had quit her job: "I'm now fully employed in the highest vocation a woman could have." Her letter conveyed her delight in caring for her two sons, channeling their curiosity to discover the wonders of nature, books, music, art, science; introducing them to God; teaching them to get along with others; giving them the security of unconditional love. This was more interesting than working on the assembly line.

Sandy knows that the actual number of hours spent with the boys is not what is most important. Family members can spend every evening in the same room ignoring or irritating one another.

She knows that children need both quantity time and quality time. Quantity time is real life—going to the grocery store, making cookies, changing the sheets, driving around town. By what she's like and how she responds to little and big crises, Sandy teaches her values to her children.

Quality time can sometimes be scheduled. A parent plans time with one child, playing ball, reading a book, going fishing or to the zoo, whatever is special to that child. But often quality time is a magic moment with the child that just happens.

I remember the day Jim brought home a print of a painting by Constable. The sun shone on the English grain field in the background. Trees shaded the brook at the edge of the field in the foreground. A Shetland sheepdog stood on the path. A little boy lay on his stomach getting a drink from the brook.

John, age three, studied the scene a long time before he said, "Let's go there." In that moment, he voiced the wish that I was too practical to speak. But he also told me volumes about himself. We hugged and wished together that we could go there. Still today, when I look at that painting, I remember that magic moment.

I'm impressed with the choices Nelda and Jack have made to limit their lifestyle so that Nelda can be at home with the children. The economic sacrifice of living on one income is consistent with their priorities. Their small, attractive house is simply and tastefully furnished; meals are economical and nutritious; they wear designer clothes from the resale shop. They enjoy free recreation in the parks, at the library, in the backyard. Jack faithfully plans time with the boys to give Nelda time for herself. They budget two luxuries, a baby sitter during their biweekly date and a week at a family camp each summer. They are building memories for their family that will be remembered more than a remodeled bathroom or an elaborate stereo system.

What about a woman's needs? Are they to be forgotten? Isn't it a priority to keep growing as a person? Certainly God wants each person to become all she can be. I'm fortunate that Jim has always encouraged me to continue to develop my talents and to learn new skills. But I've watched women like Ellen, mentioned earlier in this book, who continue to grow even without their husbands' encouragement. The church and our society provide countless opportunities for volunteers to grow and learn while they are serving others. A woman doesn't have to have a full-time job to be a growing person.

Stories from the Journey

 How freeing to know that I need to do God's will, and that's all. Not everything everyone or anyone else wants me to do . . . Not even all I want to do . . . but what he wants me to do.

Esther, 20s ■

One of my reasons for being in neighborhood Bible studies is that the weekly discussion forces me to study and think, to become a neighbor to the strangers who live down the block, and to grow spiritually. Intellectually, socially, and spiritually, I'm being stretched.

Each Christian is a unique expression of the Lord Jesus. There is something each one can do that no one else can. God has certain good works planned for each of us. I like what

Jesus said to Mary when she poured the expensive perfume on his feet (see John 12:1-8). One of the disciples criticized her for her wastefulness, but Jesus said, "Leave her alone. She has done what she could" (paraphrased).

"She has done what she could." There were lots of things Mary couldn't do, but that wasn't important. She found something she could do to express her love for Jesus. The disciple thought her action was stupid, but Jesus said she would be remembered around the world for what she did for him. I want to find what I can do to show my love for Jesus so my epitaph might be, "She has done what she could."

I want to understand myself so I can control my time to please God. I've learned that I'm a morning person. I do mental work better in the morning, but not before coffee. While I was writing this book, I blocked out each morning for writing because that's when I work best. I also wrote in the afternoons, but if I needed to visit someone or to have a committee meeting, I did it in the afternoon. You may be a night person and need to make your schedule accordingly.

The busier I am, the more lists I need. I love to scratch a completed item off the list. What a sense of accomplishment! Years ago I learned to do four things at once: brush my teeth, review the Spanish vocabulary taped to the bathroom mirror, listen to the morning news, and cajole my roommate into a happy mood before breakfast. Every woman has learned to do five things at once, or she'd never get through the day. But now I'm trying to learn to do one thing at a time. I try to finish the top item on my list before I start the next. Of course, if it is baking bread, I can do something else while the dough rises. Finishing a job gives me a sense of accomplishment and saves the time of wondering where I left off if I have to return to it.

To keep perspective on my priorities and use of time, I sometimes ask myself, *How will I be remembered thirty years from now?* I think about how I remember my parents. My strongest impressions are that they loved Jesus Christ, that they loved each other, and that they loved me. Their godly priorities determined how they spent their time and energy. And I remember them for their godliness.

Chapter Eleven

Joy Killers and Put-Downs

Along the way, the tongue

I was enjoying Sunday dinner with our friends the David-sons. Young Peter began to talk excitedly. "Dad's going to build a gazebo in the backyard, and I get to help him. We can have picnics in it and play games. Mom says I can sleep in it sometimes, too."

"But aren't the mosquitoes too bad here? We can seldom sit in our backyard in the summer without being eaten alive," I said in my most practical voice.

When I saw Peter's expression change from expectation to disappointment, I realized what I had done. With two sentences, I had killed his joy. No wonder the Bible says, "If anyone is never at fault in what he says, he is a perfect man, able to keep his whole body in check" (James 3:2).

Knowing the power of the tongue caused my friend Ruth to hang a sign on her kitchen wall, "Lord, set a guard over my lips." She had often known she needed a guard, but living with teenagers made the need critical.

Slander seems to begin at home. "You're a slob." "You can't do anything right." "Dummy." Parents and children easily attack each other with words like these.

When we told Sara and John that calling each other names and putting each other down weren't accepted in our family, they were surprised that we were upset by what they had said. John remarked, "You should hear what people say to each other at school."

I began to wonder how the cutting put-downs became so common and accepted by our teenagers. Even the third graders I was teaching in vacation Bible school were constantly putting each other down. One evening one of their remarks reminded me of a TV character in a popular sitcom. I realized that this generation was growing up listening to constant put-downs. Some were supposed to be funny, but they really hurt. They were intended to draw blood.

To control my tongue goes against my tendency to sin and against society's patterns. I do need God to guard my mouth if my words are to be godly.

Besides avoiding being a joy killer and giving put-downs, I fight the tendency to constantly correct. Jim and I became aware of this trap when we met a math professor named Tom and his wife, Nancy.

Tom was a quiet person and Nancy an extrovert. She carried most of the conversation that evening. The one time Tom told a story, she corrected every detail.

Tom: We left home at nine o'clock.

Nancy: No, it was 8:30. I remember looking at the clock as we went out the door.

Tom: We packed the car with the sleeping bags on top of the ice chest.

Nancy: No, the sleeping bags were behind the ice chest.

Tom: We reached the campground about six o'clock.

Nancy: No, don't you remember? It was almost seven because the sun was already setting.

On and on it went. We were embarrassed and ached for Tom. I wasn't surprised that after the story was finally finished, he said no more all evening.

Nagging is another trap of the tongue to avoid. I've remembered Ann Landers' definition, which I read years ago: Nagging is like being nibbled to death by a duck.

When Jim and I were first married, I told him, "I don't want to be a nagger. If you ever hear me nag, please tell me."

"I will," he promised.

Every few years, I remind him that he is to tell me, just in case he forgets. But so far he says I'm doing okay, except for asking if I'm nagging.

I realized why gossip is warned against so strongly in the Bible when I saw what it did to Barbara and Sally. One hot summer day Sally took supper to Wendy's family because Wendy was in the hospital. When Sally arrived, the kitchen was a mess. Bob had managed caring for the three children, but he couldn't get to the dishes in the sink. Sally, dressed in her tank top and cutoff jeans, tackled the dirty job and began to clean the kitchen.

Just as she finished, Bob returned from work. The children weren't home from school yet. Delighted to see a clean kitchen and smell the supper in the oven, he gave Sally a big hug.

At that moment Barbara arrived at the back door with a pie for the family. She saw Sally in Bob's arms. Why was Sally alone with Bob? Why was she dressed like that? Barbara jumped to her own conclusions: Sally was pursuing Bob while his wife was in the hospital.

Barbara knocked, gave Bob the pie, and quickly left. She didn't wait for any explanations of what she had seen. She was judge and jury of Sally and ready to deliver justice. She told her family that Sally was chasing Bob and gave them the convincing evidence. The family looked at Sally with horror and wondered how she had the nerve to teach Sunday school.

Barbara thought she should warn others to beware of Sally, and so the story spread. Soon Sally began to wonder why she was getting the cold shoulder from her fellow Christians. Finally someone mustered the courage to tell Sally the story Barbara was spreading. Sally had the painful task of confronting Barbara. As Sally told Barbara what really happened, Barbara realized the seriousness of what she had done. She had given her own meaning to what she saw without getting any facts. She had prejudged Sally's motives, and she had gossiped about them. She had not gone directly to Sally as Jesus taught us to do (see Matthew 18:15). Instead of questioning Sally's reputation, people might begin to question Barbara's credibility.

Some of the damage was repaired when Barbara asked Sally's forgiveness and made every effort not to repeat her mistake. But the tale can never be recalled.

As I guard against gossiping, I have to decide what to do when someone wants to gossip to me. The best defense I've been able to find is to immediately say something positive about the person being gossiped about. I try to put myself in that person's shoes, to think of some other explanation for the motive or action than the one being given to me.

Usually, that stops the gossiper. One woman said to me in disgust, "I guess you don't want to hear this." She was right.

Controlling my tongue isn't just stopping evil words. It also involves using words to encourage others. I want my words to nourish and to heal. "The lips of the righteous nourish many" (Proverbs 10:21), and "the tongue of the wise brings healing" (Proverbs 12:18).

Stories from the Journey

 At Pastor John's funeral, several of his grandchildren honored his memory with their tributes. They recalled Grandpa's familiar smile and greeting, "Look out, Grandma, here come the Indians." When their games collided with a vase or a window, Grandpa supervised their cleanup. But they were always reassured when they went home, "Be sure to come back soon."

One of them told about sleeping overnight on the floor at the foot of their grandparents' bed. All evening the big bedroom rang with laughter, especially Grandpa's that roared out like Niagara Falls. When he finally declared bedtime, Grandpa knelt by his bed to pray. "I tried to stay awake until he finished praying, but I could never manage it," a grandson said. "I don't know how anyone could pray so long. I think Grandpa must have fallen asleep on his knees. When we asked how he prayed so long, Grandpa said he was praying for all of us."

What wise words impressed Pastor John's grandchildren? His laughter and his prayers.

One day in our Bible study when we were discussing how we handle failure, a neighbor's nourishing words encouraged me. I told the group about feeling jealous the day before and being disgusted with myself for feeling that way.

"That was yesterday. Today is a new beginning," Hazel reminded me. "Just last week we studied what Paul said. We're to forget past failures."

I admire my mother-in-law's wise words to defuse her husband's anger. Once when Dad complained in very stormy tones about the almost-empty ketchup bottle, she smiled sweetly and said, "Why, you're right. I wonder why anyone would put that almost-empty bottle on the table when there is a full one in the cupboard." A soft answer turned anger to a thank you.

Stories from the Journey

By nature, I'm a shy, quiet person. My conscientious approach to work sent the unintentional message, "Keep your distance." One day a co-worker spoke a life-changing word to me, "I wish you would smile more." That simple request enabled me to draw closer to people, to make friends more easily, to be happier. Discovering people's needs and helping them brings me great joy. A smile still opens conversations and hearts in a retirement community as it did on the job.

Anne, 70s ■

I find both warning and comfort in the fact that God knows all about my words—the meaning behind them, my motives, my tone of voice. If I'm sarcastic, God knows it even if the person I address misses my true meaning. But if someone misjudges my motives and words, God knows what I really intend. His evaluation is the one that counts.

I needed that comfort after a faculty meeting during my first year of teaching. The principal announced a new system for collecting and accounting for the children's milk money each morning. Thinking it too complicated and time consuming, I naively suggested a simpler way. "Do you think you are experienced enough to correct me? You aren't to find fault but to do the work," he stormed back at me.

The principal considered my helpfulness to be criticism. I was crushed. But God knew my motive. I had made a stupid mistake with the principal, but I wasn't guilty before God.

I won't have perfect tongue control in this life, but with God's guard over my lips, I'm defeating joy killers, put-downs, and constant correcting, nagging, and gossiping. I'm cultivating gracious, encouraging words along the path to godliness.

Chapter Twelve

One Step Removed from Contentment

Along the way, appetites

One Wednesday night at prayer meeting when prayer requests were given, Gloria stood so that everyone could hear her. She said, "I think my house has become too important to me. God has been convicting me about the time and effort and worry I spend on it. Would you please pray for me? I want God to have first place in my life, not my house."

We prayed for Gloria as she asked us to do, and then we forgot about it. But the next Monday, we remembered. During a severe electrical storm, lightning struck her house, and the fire destroyed almost everything she owned. Gloria and lots of other people got their houses and possessions in a better perspective.

Jesus had a lot to say about our appetite for things. Being realistic about the stranglehold things can get on us, he told his followers not even to worry about having enough to eat or to wear. As an antidote to worry, he gave a promise: "But seek first his kingdom and his righteousness, and all these things will be given to you as well" (Matthew 6:33).

Jim had an early lesson in applying that promise. As a college student, he often attended Inter-Varsity meetings at the home of Mary Zimmerman, a godly woman who opened her house for students' Bible studies and for missionary speakers. One night he proudly drove his brand-new 1948 Studebaker to the meeting. As he prepared to leave, he invited Mary outside to look at his new car. She stared at it momentarily and then asked, "Is that one of those things that 'shall be added unto you'?"

Mary Zimmerman wanted to help a younger Christian to keep his possessions in the right perspective. Was Jim making possessions his goal, or was he seeking God first and then enjoying what God gave him? Some say that godliness plus riches equals contentment. But Mary Zimmerman knew that godliness plus contentment equals great gain (see 1 Timothy 6:6).

My mother-in-law provides convincing evidence about godly contentment. In December 1989, my mother-in-law had a cornea transplant to restore sight in her one good eye. A few weeks later, a broken hip hospitalized her. "Why did this happen to me? I try to live to please God," she said as we stood around her hospital bed.

An eye infection, rejection of the cornea, and glaucoma left her blind after months of anticipation of improved vision. She refused to cooperate with the physical therapist. "Why try to walk when I can't see?" she reasoned. For months she lost interest in food and in life as she mourned her losses. One day she asked Jim, "How long have I been blind?" Using that word for the first time ushered in her transition from grie acceptance.

One of her favorite activities now is the Sunday evening hymn sing for the residents in the nursing home where she lives.

Recently, I watched her sitting there in her wheelchair, wrapped in sweaters and lap robes, smiling, singing along. When the visiting leader asked for requests, Mom responded, "It Is Well with My Soul." She sang every verse from memory. That's what contentment looks like at eight-six.

Godliness with contentment keeps God first; people are to be second, and things are to be third. As I realize that everything I have comes from God and he promises to provide for all my needs, I am beginning to learn contentment. I'm glad that the apostle Paul said he *learned* contentment (see Philippians 4:11-12). It isn't something some people are born with and others aren't. It's something to be learned.

My appetite for things and the advertising industry work together against contentment. Advertisements turn wants into needs in my mind so I'll have to buy certain products. My mother thought a broom and a Bissell sweeper were all she needed to clean the floors. But we children bought her a vacuum cleaner that we thought she needed. Now I "need" two vacuum cleaners, one for carpets and one for floors.

Keeping wants from turning into needs requires resistance. It's better for me not to read the newspaper ads unless I'm looking for a specific item I need. When I realize that I do need a coat or a pair of shoes, then I begin to watch the papers for sale ads.

I've noticed that contentment is always one step removed. I think, *If I have a house, I'll be content.* We get the house.

Then I need a sofa and some carpet. With them, I'll be content. After we get the sofa and the carpet, I need new drapes. Then I'll be content. And on and on it goes. Contentment is just beyond the next item.

The size of our salary and number of possessions don't determine our contentment. When I worked for InterVarsity, I remember telling Bob, another staff worker, what a hard time I had trusting God when the checks are late and the bills are due.

To my surprise he responded, "It's harder for me to trust God when I have money in the bank. Then I trust in the bank account."

He was right. The more I have, the harder it is to remember that everything I have is from God. His good gifts are to be enjoyed. But they aren't the basis of my security or value. A person can be generous or stingy, regardless of how much money she has.

The antidote to holding on to money and the key to contentment is generous giving. That truth came home to me when we moved into our first house and the children were small. Jim thought that we should get a dishwasher. Not having to wash dishes three times a day would give me more time with the children and with our friends when we had them in for meals.

Great! I thought. So when Wanamakers had a sale, Jim stopped on his lunch hour and ordered one to be delivered the next week. The very next day, a letter arrived from the Latin America Mission about the Evangelism in Depth campaign in Honduras. To mobilize every Christian in the country to reach others with the Good News about Jesus they needed thousands of dollars. We read the letter and prayed for Honduras and the mission.

As I washed dishes the following days, I continued to pray for Honduras. The more we thought and prayed, the more we wondered if we should cancel our order for the dishwasher and give the money for Evangelism in Depth instead. That's what we did. I was delighted. Each time I washed dishes, I remembered to pray for the church in Honduras where the money originally designated for my dishwasher was helping.

At the time we didn't know we would soon move to another house and would have left the new dishwasher if we had bought it. Guess what was in the next house we bought? That's right. A dishwasher. When I held the dishwasher with an open hand, God could take it and give it back. I was twice blessed.

When we hold our possessions in an open hand, we use them without falling into the sin of loving them. We're to *love* God and people and *use* money. We need to remember that people are more important than things.

God gave me a startling reminder of that one Sunday when a family with two little girls came to dinner. I had carefully arranged the chairs so the girls would sit on the plank chairs with pads. They would be higher, and if they knelt, their shoes wouldn't scratch the better chairs without pads. While I was in the kitchen and they were being seated, somehow the children and the chairs got rearranged. The next time I dusted, I found the scratches on the good chairs. I was angry that people had been careless with *my* property. Graciously, the Lord reminded me that the chairs were one of his good gifts to use and that the people were more important than the chairs.

We gain control of our appetite for things as we get God's perspective on possessions and develop contentment. But as our possessions increase, so does our accountability. Here are some practical steps for discharging that responsibility.

First, give generously. R. G. LeTourneau, the Christian businessman and founder of a heavy machinery company, gave away 98 percent of his income after he became a millionaire. I'm sure he didn't begin giving that percentage as a young businessman, but he began giving a certain percentage. As God entrusted more to him, he gave more until he reached 98 percent.

Jim and I have practiced setting aside a percentage of our income for God every payday. In the Old Testament, Israel began with 10 percent and added offerings up to 30 percent. As God honors our faith, we've increased our giving. I recommend this to you. If your faith staggers at 10 percent, begin with 5 percent. But begin. (For more help, see *How to Give Away Your Money,* by Simon Webley.)

A seminary professor and his wife whom we know decided to live on half his salary so they could give 50 percent to the church and missions. They are willing to live simply in order to control their appetite for things. Their obvious joy in giving reflects their growing contentment.

Second, find out where the money goes. When Jim and I were first married, we kept a record for several months of how we spent every penny. Then we compared it with our budget. We had to adjust the budget to match the facts, one being that we needed more medical expenses than we had originally planned. Keeping the accounts helped us see where our money was going. We saw where we had to discipline ourselves more carefully.

Third, resist the temptation of easy credit. When we compared what we would pay for dining room furniture if we bought it on the installment plan with what we would pay in cash, we were amazed. We began saving a certain amount each month for furniture and enjoyed the interest that helped swell the account.

We have counseled couples and singles who have dug themselves into deep financial holes. Education debts are a long-range investment and may be necessary. But learning to live within your income and controlling your appetite for things are essential for contentment.

Fourth, enjoy using what God gives. Controlling our appetite for things doesn't mean we live shabbily. There is no virtue in shabbiness. God certainly approves of beauty, creativity, color, and design. Part of being made in his image is to be creative and to be able to appreciate beauty. Our churches, homes, yards, and clothing can reflect creativity and beauty. In Edith Schaeffer's book *The Hidden Art of Homemaking,* she gives delightful illustrations of using possessions to reflect God's love of beauty and love of people. Calling people to a supper table attractively set with a cloth, candles or flowers, and food that is appealing to the eye and the tongue, says something about their value.

When Diana realized that she could be forgiven, that God accepted her and Jesus died for her, she made some drastic changes in her house. She had never cared about how her house looked because she didn't think she was worth much and she felt she deserved to live in a mess. But since she realized she was someone in God's eyes, she bought new curtains and began to clean her house.

In controlling our appetite for things, we need (1) to keep a proper perspective on things as good gifts from God; (2) to learn contentment; (3) to separate wants from needs; (4) to hold possessions with an open hand; (5) to recognize my accountability for all I am given; and (6) to use money to serve God and people, including myself.

For an accurate measure of our appetite for things, consider a set of questions our pastor, Kent Hughes, gave in a sermon. He asked:

"1. What is it that occupies our thoughts when we have nothing else to do? What is it that occupies our daydreams? Is it our investments, our position? If so, those are the things we treasure, and this is where our hearts really are.

"2. What is it that we fret most about? Is it our home or our clothing? If so, then we know where our treasure lies.

"3. Apart from our loved ones, what is the thing that we dread most losing? What is it that we tremble most about?

"4. What are the things that we measure others by? (The question is a very revealing mirror because we measure other people by what we treasure.) Do we measure others by their clothing? By their education? By their homes? Or, if we are younger, by their athletic prowess? Do we measure others by their success in the business world? If so, then we know where our treasure lies.

"5. What is it that we *know* we cannot be happy without?"

The Bible warns not only against materialism but against being controlled by our physical appetites. When I was growing up, I heard lots of sermons about the evils of alcohol and tobacco. But I never heard a sermon on gluttony. When we had church suppers, our plates were heaped high with all the fried chicken, potato salad, chocolate cake, and other good things we could carry.

Today the medical profession warns us about the dangers of tobacco, alcohol, drugs, fats, caffeine, and sugar. No longer can people who don't smoke or drink but who consume twenty cups of coffee a day or live on fried foods throw stones.

Temptations differ. Jim craves a thick ham-and-cheese sandwich on two slices of pumpernickel bread. I crave apple pie or a hot fudge sundae. But the issue is, what controls me? Ham-and-cheese sandwiches and apple pie are permissible, but do they control me or do I control them?

As a youngster, I was always overweight. My friend Betty could eat anything she wanted and not gain a pound. I could smell a carrot and gain five pounds. I almost memorized the calorie book that I periodically kept by my plate. In the list of cookies, I discovered that fig bars had more calories than any other cookie. I decided that though I liked Fig Newtons, it was one food I could eliminate completely.

I didn't realize how deeply these choices were ingrained in me until one day when Sara was in junior high. She came home from school and asked, "Why don't we ever have Fig Newtons? All my friends get them in their lunch. Why can't we?"

"I just forgot they existed," I replied. She was amazed at my explanation.

Not being mastered by anything is the principle the Bible gives for controlling the appetite. Alcoholics Anonymous stresses total abstinence from alcohol for those who are controlled by it. I practice abstinence from Fig Newtons and potato chips because I can't eat just one.

Another defense against being controlled by food is fasting. Fasting doesn't win us points with God, but it brings our physical and spiritual concerns into perspective. The form of the fast doesn't really matter; it can be a total fast for a day or for one meal, or it can be a liquid diet of broth or juice.

A day of fasting and prayer at our church produced a great spiritual experience for me and others in the church. One Saturday was set aside to pray for some critical needs in the congregation and for our missionaries. The previous Sunday everyone in the congregation was encouraged to write a prayer request on a three-by-five card and bring it to the altar. In laying it there, we were committing that need to Jesus. On the Saturday we entered, we could take some of the cards from a box. We prayed for them alone, with one other person, or in small groups kneeling around the sanctuary. Then we returned the requests to another box as we left. Each request was prayed for several times during the day.

Coming to the church for the day made it easier to fast. I wasn't around any food except the container of juice I brought along. Fasting focused my attention on spiritual issues rather than on my physical comfort. I was saying to God that I did care more about the salvation of people and the reconciliation of families than about my stomach.

In the year following the day of prayer and fasting, people continued to report answers to prayer. One of the requests I had laid on the altar that morning was for my brother's salvation. Eight years later, I wrote back to the church to tell them that the prayer was answered.

In our society, controlling appetites involves drugs as well as food. Children face the temptation in elementary school. Cocaine use mounts among affluent professionals. Alcoholism among women increases. The apostle Paul warned Christians in the church in the first century not to be addicted to wine (Titus 2:3). What strong warnings he'd give us today!

Since my body is the temple of the Holy Spirit, it is possible to honor God even with my body. Part of honoring God with my body is not being controlled by any food or drug.

Many people, including myself, need to control the amount of sleep we get. When I was in school, I had to put the alarm clock across the room so I had to get out of bed to turn it off. Otherwise, I could turn it off in my sleep and never know it. Some friends never went to bed, cheating themselves of the sleep they needed. Some people are day people; some are night people. The battle of getting up in the morning is won or lost the night before.

The ability to control our appetites is part of the fruit of the Holy Spirit! We don't have to lick them by ourselves. As God makes us more like Jesus, he builds in self-control. That includes control of your unique, hard-to-control appetites, whatever they may be. Jesus in you is stronger than any of them.

Stories from the Journey

I'm learning that we are each on our own path to godliness.

My path has things on it that are meant and needed for my growth and no one else's. Now when I look at other Christians who have accomplished a lot, instead of wishing that I could be "as smart as . . ." "as talented as . . ." "as gifted as . . ." etc., I can praise God for them and let it be. I can walk my path, content with being who God made me and the path laid out for me.

Sylvia, 40s, mother of two ■

Chapter Thirteen

Idealism, Realism, and What's Really Happening

Along the way, anger

At nine o'clock on Sunday morning, I finished helping Sara dress and sent her downstairs. Then I hastily dressed John while I kept an eye on the clock. I still had to finish dressing myself and get out the door by 9:15 for Sunday school.

"If only I had six hands, all three of us might be ready on time," I told myself wishfully.

Just then Jim called from downstairs, "I'm going for a walk, and I'll take Sara along."

He's going for a walk! I repeated to myself in disbelief. *I'm getting three people dressed, I have cooked breakfast and washed the dishes, and all he is interested in is going for a walk. How can he be so selfish? What have I gotten myself into?* My blood pressure rose thirty points, my stomach knotted, and my tears flowed.

131

After several Sundays of this disastrous pattern, Jim said, "I think we need to talk about why you're in tears every Sunday morning. Is there some way I can help you?"

"I'm in tears because I have three people to get ready and you have only one. I like to fix a nice breakfast because it's one morning you don't leave early for the train. But you are just interested in having a walk before you go to church," I blurted out between gulps for self-control.

"I only went for a walk to help you. I thought that taking Sara out would free you to take care of John," he said slowly.

"But I was so hurt and angry because I thought you were just thinking about yourself," I timidly admitted.

"It sounds as if we need to change something. Would it help you if I cook breakfast on Sunday morning while you get the children ready?" he offered.

"I guess I thought a wife should serve an ideal family breakfast on Sunday morning as well as do everything else. That wasn't very smart, was it?" I confessed with great relief. "I'd love for you to be in charge of Sunday breakfast."

Thus began the Sunday cheese omelet breakfast tradition at the Reapsomes, which continued for eleven years until Jim became a pastor. By then the rest of us could help him on Sunday morning.

I learned some important lessons from these painful mornings:

1. *Don't judge the other person's motives.* I'd judged Jim's motives and ascribed the worst possible reasons for his behavior.

2. *Say how you feel.* I hadn't told Jim how I felt. I just nursed my hurt and let my anger grow.

3. *Don't try to change the other person.* I kept wishing Jim would change. But it didn't occur to me to think about changing the situation.

I hadn't yet learned the basic principle: " 'In your anger do not sin': Do not let the sun go down while you are still angry, and do not give the devil a foothold" (Ephesians 4:26-27).

Realizing that anger itself is not sin is a great liberation. It is what we do with anger that can be sin. Jesus was angry about how the money changers were abusing the temple. He was angry about people's stubborn hearts and their lack of compassion. God is angry about sin.

If we think anger is always a sin, we may deny that we're angry. I remember hearing a panel of mothers talking about parenting. One woman, the mother of seven and therefore an expert, said, "I never allow my children to be angry."

I was too young and inexperienced to know what was wrong with that statement, but I didn't think it sounded right. Now I understand what she meant: "I don't allow my children to express their anger." She couldn't stop how they felt, but she could stop them from showing their feelings.

Emotions are a normal part of being made in the image of God. God expresses the whole range of emotions: love, hate, compassion, anger, jealousy, sorrow, grief. Remembering this helps me accept my emotions and learn to recognize them.

Stories from the Journey

 I recognize my anger. Now what? I can't just say, "O.K. That hurt but I'll forget it." The church my husband pastors planned to send us to Asia to visit some of our missionaries.

For years we've dreamed of being able to see missions firsthand, to increase our own understanding and to encourage our missionaries. Friends and family arranged to care for our children. Our anticipation soared like a hot air balloon with every welcoming letter from the missionaries. Our hope crash-landed at the annual business meeting. The recession cancelled our trip and our cost-of-living raise!

Why us? I cried to myself and to God. Disappointed hope doesn't just smilingly accept economic realities. As I poured out my anger to God, I began to see that all of our family's needs had been met. Without the raise, we still had everything we needed. God comforted me as I mourned our losses. As I got his perspective, I could put my anger to rest.

Denise, 40s, mother of three ■

Sometimes I'm slow at figuring out what my feelings are. I was angry at Jim when he went for a walk on Sunday morning. But it took me awhile to figure out why I was angry. Behind the anger was the fear that he didn't care about me, that he was going to take care of himself and leave me to do the same.

After I understood why I was angry, I saw that I'd been judging his motives. I hadn't given him the benefit of the doubt. No wonder Jesus said that if you think someone has offended you, go and talk to him about it (see Matthew 18:15).

When we did talk, I saw how groundless my fears were. Jim was trying to help me all along. We needed to work out a solution by changing our routine, not by my changing him.

Part of my anger came from my unrealistic ideal of the perfect wife. Because I couldn't serve the perfect breakfast in a perfectly calm, relaxed manner and dress two children and myself on time to walk out the door as the perfect family should, I felt guilty. It was false guilt, but it stung. When I recognized my idealism, I could accept the truth and allow Jim to give me the help he had always been willing to give.

But I also had real guilt. I had falsely accused my husband. I had to admit that to him and ask his forgiveness. Then I asked God's forgiveness.

If I had not let the sun go down on my anger, I could have saved us weeks of frustration. Instead of suffering silently, nursing my anger, I could have been enjoying the cheese omelets and the closeness to Jim that I wanted.

Maybe you've fallen into some destructive traps. Frequent articles in women's magazines warn of illness or depression that hidden anger produces. The mother I mentioned, who wouldn't allow her children to be angry, suffered from severe back problems. I often wondered if that was where her anger settled.

Another poor way to handle anger is for one person to talk only about facts while the other talks about feelings. The two can never hear each other because they are talking different languages.

When Jim and I discussed the Sunday morning fiasco, I told him I felt deserted. I was afraid he cared only about

himself and not about helping me. That's talking feelings. If
he had come back with a list of everything he had ever done
to help me to show how illogical I was being, it would not
have helped. I didn't need logic. I needed him to do what he
did—listen to how I felt.

Stories from the Journey

 I long for peace and tranquility. I want my home
to be a place of calmness and serenity. But when
I'm uptight and frazzled, the family absorbs my
turmoil. The calmer I am, the calmer everyone else seems to
be. Sometimes I resent that my family drains me emotionally
until I remember God's unlimited supply of calm. My problem is, I forget to refill my cup at the well.

Joann, 40s, mother of two ■

Enough about the destructive ways to handle anger. We are
all too familiar with them. How can I handle anger in a godly
way? How can I be angry without sinning?

One constructive way to defuse anger is to talk to an objective third party who can help identify the real cause of the
anger. This needs to be done in confidence and not with
someone who will tell me I am all right and the other person
all wrong. This third party is a safety valve to help me verbal-
ize my feelings and get perspective.

I play the role of the third party for Margie, who is constantly frustrated by her boss's lack of communication. She

needs information from him to complete her work. She hates to keep asking for it and getting another empty promise that she'll get it "today."

As she told me about the problem, we tried to think of reasons why he might behave as he does. He is new in his job. He appears very unsure of himself, having to check and recheck things before he can pass them on. He may be overloaded and hasn't figured out the priority to give her requests.

Thinking about the problem from his point of view defused her anger. Margie began to look for ways to affirm him in some way. She looked for anything she could thank him for. She asked how things were going for him. Was there anything she could do to help him get to the papers she needed? Talking about the problem helped Margie discover new ways to look at her boss and their problem.

Another tool for handling anger constructively is physical activity. Taking a vigorous walk, working in the garden, or kneading bread clears my thinking and relaxes my tight muscles. Working out my frustrations on the weeds or dough defuses my anger and gives me time to figure out the real issue.

Sometimes a little time and distance spare us from serious regrets. One day as Jim mowed the lawn, he ran over the clippers John had left at the edge of the bushes. Bang! A badly damaged mower blade. A very angry father. By the time John got home several hours later, Jim had thought several dozen times about what he needed to say to John. But he also had time to cool off and be glad for what he didn't say.

Good use of anger can change situations and solve problems. Some people got angry enough about slavery to bring it to an end. Some are using anger against wife and child abuse to provide shelters and counseling. Some have brought changes in nursing homes and jails because of their anger over poor conditions.

As part of godliness, we need to recognize our emotions, accept them, and learn how to use them for good. We can choose to use our anger constructively or destructively. If we really blow it, hurting ourselves and others with our anger, we need to bring it to God for his help. As a choir director advised, "If you girls will sing the wrong notes, I can help you. But if you don't sing, I can't help you."

Chapter Fourteen

I Feel . . . I Wish . . . I Want . . .

Along the way, confronting

I'd never thought of confronting as a positive skill to be learned until I read *Caring Enough to Confront* by David Augsburger. By nature, I choose peace at any price. Not rocking the boat appeals to me more than confronting. My silence isn't golden; it's yellow.

Karen isn't a boat rocker either. She grew up in a home in which she never saw her parents disagree or raise their voices. As far as she knew, life was always peaceful between a husband and a wife who loved each other. She was unprepared for her husband Allen's outspokenness about *everything*. At his home, everyone said what he or she thought; all grievances were aired. He assumed all families behaved that way.

After six months of life with Allen, Karen wanted to either kill him or divorce him, but she knew both options were out.

She would have to learn to fight with him. So she bought a book on how to fight with the man you love. It saved her sanity and their marriage.

Karen discovered that conflicts are inevitable. They happen at home, at work, at church, in the neighborhood. We all develop ways to avoid or handle them. Confronting is a constructive way to manage conflicts.

Confronting is one of the skills Karen learned. The Bible tells us to speak the truth in love (see Ephesians 4:15). That's what I mean by confronting. When I speak in truth, I say what I really think. I say what I really feel. If I don't speak, I brood over the matter and let it grow out of proportion. Speaking the truth in love isn't attacking or accusing the other person.

One fall I was so pleased with myself for baking a pumpkin pie for Jim before he asked for one. As I smelled it cooking in the oven, I anticipated his smile and pleasure when I served it at supper. But my happy anticipation turned to instant self-pity. While the pie cooled on the counter, Jim passed through the kitchen and glanced at it.

"You burned the crust," he reported like a teacher returning my spelling test.

How dare he be so ungrateful! How could he say such a thing when I took the trouble to make his favorite pie? These and a dozen other accusations raged in my head as I stood dumbfounded.

Should I just be hurt and let that remark ruin my day? Should I attack him? Or should I try confronting?

Gathering up my courage and creativity, I said with a smile, "You mean, 'How nice you baked a pumpkin pie.'"

We both laughed and the anticipated thank-you kiss and hug arrived on the spot, better than express mail.

Another time it was my turn to be on the receiving end. As Jim and I talked with friends after church, I made a very poor attempt at humor about something that really wasn't funny.

Once we were alone in the car, Jim said gently, "I hope you don't say anything like that again." In a flash I saw what a foolish and potentially damaging remark I had made. Chagrined, I thanked him for not being quiet but speaking the truth in love.

Stories from the Journey

 Everyone on the block knew that Ed had a drinking problem. As I got to know his wife, Eileen, the trauma and anger of thirty years of living with an alcoholic poured out like water over a broken dam. Insults, embarrassments, tantrums, accidents, and disappointments fueled her anger and hostility toward him.

"He says he doesn't need help, that nothing is wrong with him," Eileen shouted. "I get so mad, I'd like to kill him."

"Have you seen the ads on TV about intervention?" I asked cautiously. "They show children reading letters to their daddy telling that they love him but want to run away when he is drinking."

"It wouldn't do any good; Ed would never go. He doesn't think he has a problem."

"Then maybe you need help to learn how to cope. Have you ever visited an Al-Anon meeting for families of an alcoholic?" I responded.

"Yes, I went once, but never again. One woman just shouted and cursed the whole time," she countered.

For months I prayed, befriended, listened. Finally I realized that constant reruns of this conversation were pointless.

One day when Eileen complained again that Ed wouldn't go for help, I gathered up my courage, took a deep breath and said, "You criticize Ed for saying he doesn't need help. But what you are doing is worse. You told me that you know you need help. Yet you won't do anything to get it."

Shocked but silent, she shook her head.

"You know about intervention. When you are ready to do something, you call me and I'll help you make an appointment," I promised.

About six weeks later, Eileen called. "I'm ready. Would you go with me to make arrangements for an intervention?"

Ed entered a treatment center the day of the intervention.

Five anniversaries of Ed's new beginning have dispelled my fear of loving confrontation.

Viola, 60s ■

Sometimes I'm not willing to confront. I prefer pretending nothing is wrong just to keep peace. That's what Alice did when Harry called for the fourth night in row to say he'd be late for supper. His long, last-minute apologies didn't make matters any better.

"It's okay, Honey. No problem," she replied sweetly while the knots tightened in her stomach.

If she had spoken the truth in love, she might have said, "It's not okay. I have special things planned. I want time with you. I feel as if your customers are more important to you than I am."

That would be saying what she thought and felt. No trapping questions such as, "Why do you always call me at the last minute?" No old grievances such as, "And you forgot my birthday last month, too."

Confronting is communicating feelings without insulting or attacking the other person. No "you . . ." statements, but "I . . ." statements—"I feel . . . , " "I wish . . . ," "I want . . ."

Nancy hasn't learned to confront one of the women at work who keeps asking her for more and more favors. Nancy usually replies, "Sure, no bother at all. Anything for a friend."

But inside, she resents being used. "I wish they'd lean on someone else. I act like Miss Sweetness and get stomach acid."

Nancy could sweeten the relationship if she told her friend something like, "Sorry, but I can't help this time. I have all I can handle today."

At middle age, my friend Shirley is learning how to confront her father. She's lived all her life in the shadow of his incessant complaints and his selfishness, as her mother did until her early death. In one of her colorful letters, she told me about the day she took him to the ophthalmologist.

Stories from the Journey

 It was a beautiful fall day. I prayed beforehand! He was just getting started on one of his tirades when I said quite firmly that he had always been too critical of people, and it was a shame that though the Lord let him live to be eighty years old, it still wasn't long enough for him to have out-grown that unfortunate habit. There was a brief period of utter silence. Then other things were spoken of.

After seeing the doctor, I took him on a long drive around to see some of the new housing projects, then a long drive out into the country, east of town. He perked up and exclaimed about this and that. Only when he was about to nod did I take him home.

"Did you have a good time?" I chirped when we returned. He admitted that he did, ate lunch, and bumbled off to take a nap. It was rather a good day.

Shirley, 50s ■

Shirley's courage to speak the truth in love saved the day for both of them. She went home without any anger or indigestion. Her father went home with happy memories and some new ideas to ponder about himself and God.

144

Stories from the Journey

I'm thankful for the people who modeled confronting for me.

My therapist convinced me I am not responsible for other people's feelings and that my feelings are valuable and worth attending to. Getting angry doesn't have to be unfair, blaming, and abusive. Communicating anger is like saying, "Ouch! Hey, get off my toe," when you're stepped on.

Watching a couple I respect interact with each other helped also. When the husband interrupted his wife, she let him know she didn't appreciate it and continued with her story. There were sparks in the air, but the atmosphere wasn't poisoned.

I've learned that a confrontation can improve a relationship if the confronter cares about the other person and reflects her perceptions rather than making dogmatic statements. The other person can recognize the truth.

Recently I chose to confront an underperforming young coworker, knowing she had been under fire for her high volume of mistakes. She wants to do a good job but keeps coming up short.

Over lunch, I didn't say, "I know how you feel." Rather, I told her that I hadn't been sent to talk to her, but felt I could identify with her. I described my struggles with anxiety over not being able to keep up with expectations. My efforts to please were never good enough. Counseling helped me to develop more realistic expectations and to recognize my value. I wanted her to know that help is available.

Though she wasn't verbal about her feelings, her blush and the tone of her voice assured me she was touched that someone cared about her. "You're right about my anxiety, but I didn't know that it showed."

Later that afternoon her supervisor asked for a report due the next day. Instead of her usual pattern of lengthy apologies and explanations, she simply said, "I have the report at home. Would you like me to get it now or bring it tomorrow?"

As I commended her calm, direct response our trust level grew. Confrontation can improve a relationship.

Carol Joy, 30s ■

Not confronting involves the risk of bitterness as I hide my true feelings, or the risk of erecting walls one brick at a time by little, unresolved hurts. Confronting also involves taking a risk and being vulnerable. When I share my true feelings, the other person may use the information against me. But speaking the truth in love can open a level of intimacy we never dreamed possible.

Chapter Fifteen

It's All Right to Need Other People

Along the way, interdependence

When I met Shirley in college, one of the first things I noticed about her was her determination not to need anyone. She prided herself on being five feet of total independence. Tough, self-contained, determined, she didn't allow many people behind her protective wall.

Because of her multitude of medical problems, her father considered her an inconvenience and told her so. (This is the man she has learned to confront after his eighty years of complaining.) As a child, extensive lung surgery forced her to spend months in a rehabilitation center far from home. Her mother, a tiny, frail, gentle woman, the only person who loved her, could seldom come to visit. Shirley struggled with resentment toward her uncaring father. Not wanting anyone to see her loneliness and feel sorry for her, she built thick walls around herself to shut out anyone who might discover she was vulnerable and hurt her more.

Early in her teaching career, Shirley allowed a crack in the wall. A little, brown-eyed, cheery, six-year-old girl from an orphanage slipped through the crack into Shirley's heart. Each holiday and summer vacation Debbie spent with Shirley widened the opening in the wall. As Shirley allowed herself to love Debbie, she discovered it's all right for people to need each other. In loving she took a risk. Debbie could return her love or reject it. When Shirley became Debbie's foster parent, they became vulnerable by needing each other.

Today Shirley is recovering from taking that risk. (I'll tell you the details of that deep hurt in the chapter on forgiveness.) But she has learned to love. She knows people need each other. When she considers rebuilding her wall, another needy child appears who is worth a risk.

I've watched Shirley learn that she really needs other people and that it isn't a sign of weakness but just how God made her. She isn't intended to be a self-contained island. To be human is to need others; we need to love and be loved. Maybe that's why the chief commandments are to love God and to love one another.

Part of godliness is learning to give and receive love. Jesus knew how to do both but without an unhealthy dependence on others. He needed his friends, but he didn't expect them to meet all his needs.

Cathy had that mistaken expectation about friends. She was just recovering from a divorce when we met. At eighteen, she had married a very domineering man, several years older than she was. Now, at thirty, she was on her own for the first time in her life. She had gone from dependence on her parents to dependence on her husband. She expected other people to make decisions for her and tell her what to do. But now there was no one to do that. About the same time as the divorce, she became a Christian. She thrived on God's love and forgiveness. She joined a church and attached herself to a few people and the pastor. But eventually the church split, and the pastor moved away. Just as she was finding new people on whom to be dependent, they disappeared. She found another church and looked for friends. But she was still looking for friends who would tell her how to live her life.

At work, Cathy's supervisor was her role model, a gracious, mature woman whom she admired. Having Donna's approval and friendship was the most important thing about going to work. Just when Cathy felt Donna was becoming her friend as well as her supervisor, Donna was transferred to Florida. Cathy was devastated. Every time she found someone to lean on, the person left.

"God, what are you trying to tell me?" she cried. God answered her with reassurance that she could lean on him. He wouldn't move or be transferred. He wouldn't be too busy for her. But neither did he want her to allow others to do for her what he wanted to do.

"I'm learning to turn to God more quickly," Cathy told me. "It's just so new for me to think that God has completely accepted me and wants to be my friend.

"I've learned to ask, 'What does God want me to do?' but I still have trouble asking, 'What do I want to do?' I've never asked that. I just did what I thought others expected."

She has isolated herself from the other women at work because of their different personalities and lifestyles. She has criticized and resented them, even though she knows they need the spiritual life she has. She has reacted to them—their behavior has determined her behavior.

Recently, Cathy came to report a breakthrough. She said, "I had never put together the rejection I feel from the divorce and the women at work with the acceptance I know I have from God. But Sunday when we talked about the two together, I realized that I don't need to react to their moods. I am accepted by God. What more do I need? So today when I went in to work, I smiled and said good morning to everyone. They actually smiled back."

Cathy is moving from being dependent on people to being dependent on God. She's learning to make healthy friendships rather than demand more than people can give. Instead of expecting one person to meet *all* her needs, she's making friends with older women, families, and her peers.

She is learning to give as well as take. She tried helping in the Sunday school at different age levels until she found where she was comfortable. To her delight, she discovered that the four-year-old kids like getting hugs and sitting on the teacher's lap.

In letters to a friend, Cathy is being more open about herself and the changes God is bringing in her life. The friend responds with questions about Cathy's faith and her own struggles. As a result, Cathy sees that others also need her.

Shirley is learning it's all right to need other people. It isn't weak and unspiritual, just part of being human. Cathy is learning it's good to be needed. We're created needing to give. We walk the path to godliness dependent on God and still needing friends.

Stories from the Journey

 No one has to convince me that God created us to need one another. His supporting cast for me includes loving parents, grandparents, aunts, uncles, a sister, teachers, friends, husband, in-laws, children, pastors. In my darkest crisis, facing a divorce I didn't want, God miraculously directed me to a very wise priest whose counsel provided the insights and encouragement I desperately needed. My supportive family, a weekly Bible study group, and other Christian friends prayed and encouraged me through the trauma. My two-year-old son, Jimmy, motivated me to keep functioning when I wanted to quit.

Now, years later, God gives me opportunities to befriend women enduring similar pain. Especially at work, as I pray and watch for hurting people, conversations open.

"But it's lonely on the job," I complained to God last year.

Then I received an offer to transfer to another department. I struggled with leaving people open to talking about spiritual issues but finally accepted the new position.

Imagine my delight in meeting my replacement. Cindy, a winsome disciple of Jesus, continues the witness in that office.

God knew I needed a prayer partner in the work place. Cindy's cheery yellow note pad with a smiling face above "This is the day the Lord has made; let us rejoice and be glad in it," dispels my loneliness on the job. Getting a call from Cindy at the end of a *bad* day is like God's calling to say, "I care about how you're doing today."

Marilyn, 40s, mother of two ■

Sometimes I've had problems being a friend to someone who wanted to be dependent on me. I'm not anyone's messiah. I know I can't allow someone to be dependent to feed my ego needs.

Mary Beaton, an InterVarsity staff worker at summer camp, set a good example I've tried to follow. Once a distraught student awakened Mary about 3:00 A.M. crying, "Mary, I have to talk to you. There is no God. He isn't there."

"Yes, there is a God, June. We'll talk about him in the morning. Go back to bed," Mary responded calmly and then went back to sleep. She firmly maintained, "Discussions are pointless after midnight." Her steady faith in the face of hysteria helped others to take hope but didn't make them dependent on her.

Another staff worker, Fred, told about the day he brought his wife and baby home from the hospital. A student he had been helping for several months showed up at his door.

"I have to talk to you," she pleaded anxiously. "I hitchhiked all morning to get here. You're the only one I know who can help me."

Frantically, Fred weighed his options. He knew his first responsibility at that moment was to his family. The student was upset, but she could wait until the next morning. Her problem hadn't happened overnight, and it wouldn't be solved overnight.

When they met the next day, the young woman confided, "Your turning me away yesterday forced me to go to God. There wasn't anyone else left. I have resisted facing God directly with my needs. Thanks for pushing me."

Besides being interdependent as human beings, Christians are interdependent as members of the body of Christ. Each

Christian expresses Christ in a unique way and has gifts the rest of us need (see Romans 12:4-8).

Mutual care and encouragement in the church have been such a help to me that I was shocked by a junior-high Sunday school class I was teaching one Sunday. We were studying 1 Corinthians 12, which compares the church to a physical body. Every part needs every other part. If one part hurts, all the rest of the parts suffer, too. If one part is happy or honored, all the other parts are happy, too.

Larry responded quickly, "That's not true. If I get hurt, nobody cares."

The whole class agreed. Not one of them had ever seen Christians caring about their pain. I could have been talking about life on the moon. They looked at me in total disbelief. I still hurt when I remember that day.

But I have seen members of the body show their mutual love and care for one another. In one church, the Sunshine Committee takes special care of the widows of the church. Several times a year a luncheon is held for them. The committee sends cards and gifts on special occasions. If a widow is ill and needs transportation to the doctor or needs the roof repaired or the leaves raked, the committee is there to help. One young man has taken the instructions about the care of widows in 1 Timothy 5 as his personal ministry. He washes windows, digs flower beds, and paints for widows who don't have family to help them.

Another church has Encourage One Another cards in the pew. I can write a note on the card, put the person's name on the back, and drop it in the offering plate. On Monday, the church secretary addresses and mails them. Seeing the card reminds me of my opportunity to encourage someone. I hope

my card does for my friend what Job's words did according
to Job 4:4: "Your words have supported those who stumbled;
you have strengthened faltering knees."

A Sunday school class sent Teri and Steve to a hotel for a
weekend while another couple kept their children. They couldn't
afford any time for just the two of them, and their marriage
was showing the strain.

Stories from the Journey

 How do I feel so secure in God's love and acceptance of me when my friends don't? I got a clue
from counting the godly influences I've enjoyed:
(1) My parents' words and example taught me that living to
please God was their highest joy; (2) Sunday school teachers
modeled the truths they taught and helped me work out the
application in my life; (3) Especially during high school, my
fun loving friends encouraged one another to keep our lives
pure; (4) Daily, the Holy Spirit reminds me of God's instructions and tells me how to repent when I've made wrong
choices.

Judi, 20s, mother of two ■

Helen, a widow in the church, has found her way to be an
encourager. She writes notes regularly to each shut-in, to
missionaries and their children, and to others who might be
overlooked. While I was writing this book, my computer

broke. Friends gave me a house key and the use of their computer while they were at work each day.

One day when my prayer partner came to our house, I noticed her winter coat was wearing thin and was obviously very old. For days I thought about the coat because I knew she couldn't afford to buy one. I was sure God wanted me to buy her a coat. So I decided to send her a check for a hundred dollars. That day as I was cleaning out an old chest, I found an envelope that I didn't remember putting there. In the envelope were two fifty-dollar government bonds. When I asked Jim about the bonds, he didn't remember our having them either. But we agreed that cleaning out a chest on that day and finding the bonds was a Coincidence with a capital C.

The next Sunday Sylvia was wearing a beautiful, warm, red wool coat. As we laughed together over the joy of giving and receiving, she said, "Would you believe this $240 coat was on sale yesterday for $100?"

That time I was on the giving end, but often I've been on the receiving end. When a farmer in the church lost his corn crop to a hail storm, we wept with him and his family and gave. Years later we were on the receiving end from them when we needed it.

In the church, each member has a gift to use for the good of the other members. The pastoral staff are to train us and help us, but caring for one another is the responsibility of all the members (see Ephesians 4:11-13).

Sometimes I have trouble serving another person because she is very different from me. Ann thinks differently from the way I do. She pushes for different things to happen. I'm tempted to think of her as my enemy. In reality she is a member of the same body, an arm or a foot that I need although I don't see how at the moment. As long as I focus on our differences, I'm fighting her. I forget that the real battle is against Satan. I have to ask God to help me see Ann as my sister and Satan as the enemy.

One of my favorite ways of showing my care for others is offering hospitality. Christians are commanded to offer hospitality to one another. I've never heard a sermon on that command, but it is repeated several times (see Romans 12:13; Titus 1:8; 1 Peter 4:9). Any member of the body, single or married, can serve another in this way. An apartment can be just as warm and inviting as a house, and a simple supper of sandwiches can be just as delightful as a buffet dinner if the host or hostess has the proper attitude.

I must confess that I had to unlearn some ideas about hospitality. After we had had a perfectly served steak dinner at Nadyne's house, I returned the invitation. The day before they came, I polished the silver, shopped, and began the cleaning. The next morning I made the yeast rolls and sour cream apple pie, finished the cleaning, ironed the tablecloth, set the table, and worried about the correct time to start the roast and vegetables. That was the day our Shetland sheepdog, Fancy, found a pile of dog manure to roll in. As she ran past me into the house, I got a whiff. Why, of all the days to find it, was it today! Washing the dog wasn't on my schedule. By the time the guests arrived, I was exhausted. My interest in them and their conversation was overshadowed by my wanting their approval and acclaim for the perfect dinner I served and the perfect house I kept. When I thought about that evening later, I realized I had been competing with Nadyne as a hostess. I wasn't offering hospitality; I was trying to "entertain" my guests.

Later I read Karen Mains's book *Open Heart—Open Home*, and found a kindred spirit. She added to my resolve to change. I have learned to simplify the menu and to let people bring a salad or a dessert. If the house isn't perfect, it's all right. The guests are coming not to inspect my housekeeping but to visit. I can listen to them and enjoy our conversation because I'm not exhausted from hours of preparation.

Stories from the Journey

Hospitality—from a threat to a joy. All the years I focused on my fears and insecurities, I dreaded having guests. I needed to learn to accept myself and become comfortable with who I am.

As my confidence in God's acceptance grows, I'm free to focus on my guests and how to make them comfortable.

Karen, 40s ■

At different stages in my life, hospitality has taken different forms, but it has always been a part of my life. Including a friend at Tuesday night supper gives me and my family opportunities to be encouragers, to see what God is doing in another person, and to share what Jesus has done for us. The friend is usually a single man or woman who appreciates a home-cooked meal and conversation with Christians. Some have never been a part of a Christian home and have never watched people disagree with one another and still be friends. Others are far away from family and love being included.

As a pastor's wife, I often served eight to twelve people a Sunday dinner of beef stew, gelatin salad, hot biscuits, and a simple dessert. Even men who thought meat and potatoes always had to be separate liked it. The stew cooked while we were in church; the salad and the dessert were made on Saturday. I could enjoy offering hospitality and getting better acquainted with church families because I had time to enjoy the get-togethers.

Offering hospitality doesn't have to mean serving dinner. A friend invited us to Saturday morning breakfast on a cold winter morning. We enjoyed looking at the winter wonderland through the big window by the table. An evening of games and dessert, a lunch of canned soup and fruit, a cup of tea, and a bed to a traveler are all ways of practicing hospitality.

Stories from the Journey

 I'm getting up the courage to invite some friends over for "popcorn and praise!" I tend to make hospitality more complicated than fun.

Mary, 30s, pastor's wife, mother of two ■

Shirley and Cathy learned about interdependence between people as fellow human beings. I gave examples of interdependence in the church as members of one body. Now let's consider how interdependence works out in marriage.

Chapter Sixteen

Keeping It All in Balance

*Along the way, interdependence
in marriage*

If I ever doubt that opposites attract, I think about Harry and Marsha. Harry is the serious, analytical type who plans ahead and is superorganized in his work, his gardening, and his study. Marsha is the bubbling people person, accepting everyone with open arms, going spontaneously on a wildflower or bird walk. Years ago they worked as single missionaries with North Africa Mission in different countries.

Their wise supervisor saw the possibilities of matchmaking. What a combination: seriousness balanced with laughter, spontaneity balanced with some organization. A man and a woman, each a whole person in Jesus Christ, but as husband and wife a complement to each other.

The supervisor was right. Today Harry and Marsha manage one of the mission's centers for training new missionaries. They are able to do as a couple what they couldn't have done singly. God is using their differences to bring out the best in the other and make each one more like the Lord Jesus. That's what it means for a husband and a wife to be interdependent.

Marsha doesn't need a husband to make her a whole person. She's already whole in Jesus Christ. No man, home, career, or children could make her whole. But she and Harry can each be the complement the other needs to become all God wants them to be.

In the Garden of Eden, Adam named the animals as they paraded by. With every passing pair, his loneliness must have intensified. Every creature in the garden had a companion except him. He was alone. For the first time, God declared something in creation as "not good": "It is not good for the man to be alone. I will make a helper suitable for him" (Genesis 2:18).

So God created Eve, also an expression of his image but not identical to Adam, to complement Adam and be the companion he needed. They enjoyed oneness and openness with each other as no humans have enjoyed since. They had nothing to hide, no sin to cover, no competition, no selfishness. They enjoyed God and creation. But sin came, and the barriers went up. Guilt, shame, blame, hiding, covering up, lying. Adam and Eve reaped the consequences of sin: pain, domination, hard labor, death.

Then Jesus died to restore fellowship with God and relationships between people. As we let God make us more like Jesus, we come closer to enjoying the companionship Adam and Eve first had. It won't ever be perfect because we are marred by sin, but it can get better every year.

Earlier, I talked about people needing people because God made us that way; then I talked about Christians needing one another because we are members of his body. Now let's see how needing others works out in marriage.

For years I listened to sermons on Paul's instructions in Ephesians 5; "wives, submit to your husbands" usually got twenty-five minutes, and "husbands, love your wives" got five minutes. Then Jim and I were asked to speak to a couples' class on this passage. When we began to look at the passage in the context of the whole book of Ephesians, we discovered the basic principle for Christians relating to one another: "Submit to one another out of reverence for Christ" (Ephesians 5:21).

Between husband and wife, parents and children, slaves and masters (employees and employers), God asks for *mutual submission*. Being filled with the Holy Spirit is to result in

- addressing one another with psalms
- singing and making melody
- giving thanks
- submitting to one another.

This is addressed to all Christians, regardless of sex or rank.

How does mutual submission work out in daily living between husband and wife? One of the first ways Jim and I experienced it was in learning to work together. After we moved into our first house, I eagerly planned the flower garden I'd plant if the snow ever melted. One Sunday afternoon I brought my plans to Jim, expecting him to be as excited about zinnias and cosmos as I was.

161

His response was something like, "Fine. Tell me when it's finished." Crushed, I quietly slipped upstairs to cry. How could this wonderful man I had married refuse to help me? Granted, I hadn't actually asked him for help, but surely he knew I wanted us to do it together.

Later when I came downstairs and the football game was over, he asked me what was wrong. I had learned that it was better to say what bothered me. If I said, "Oh, nothing's wrong," frustration grew and anger set in.

"I was hurt that you won't help me make a flower garden," I managed between breaths to control my tears.

"I didn't know you wanted my help," he said in honest surprise. "You told me what you were going to do, and I said, 'Fine.' Do you want me to help?"

"Of course, I want you to help. The fun will be doing it together, not by myself," I replied with great relief.

So we began learning to garden together by moving bushes, planting new ones, weeding, and enjoying the results. When we moved to a house on a larger lot, Jim began a vegetable garden. Without planning it, we fell into the pattern of my caring for the flowers and Jim's caring for the vegetables. We eagerly share spring digging and planting, warfare against rabbits and bugs, and the pleasure of feasting our eyes and our stomachs on the fruit of our labors.

Sometimes working together can make mutual frustration. There was a time when I tried to use a roller to paint the bedroom. I put paint in all the places it wasn't supposed to be and very little where I wanted it. Now Jim paints the walls, and I paint the woodwork.

162

Another expression of mutual submission is encouraging each other. On our twenty-second anniversary, I made a pot of vegetable soup and some homemade bread for a special lunch. I set the table with extra care. At eleven o'clock I took a neighbor to the doctor to have the cast checked on her arm. The cast wasn't fitting properly so it had to be removed and more x-rays made. By the time I got home, Jim had finished lunch and returned to the office.

But there on the kitchen table at my place was a note written in capital letters:

SUPER SOUP
SUPER WIFE
SUPER 22 YEARS

Submission works in making decisions about how we use our money and time. For exercise and relaxation, Jim enjoys playing golf and fishing. I enjoy bird watching and going to museums. We budget money for his golf games and an annual rendezvous with two of his fishing friends. We also budget for my annual membership to the arboretum and bird watching classes.

Of course, no two people always reach agreement. Sometimes we talk and talk and still differ on a decision. In mutual submission, we wait, think, and pray separately. But consensus may not occur. Then what?

Since the husband is the head of the wife, the buck stops with him. He is responsible to God for his leadership and decision making. So after giving all my input, praying, and trusting God to give Jim wisdom, I rest with Jim's decision. That means that neither of us will say later, "I told you so" or "If only we had done it my way."

In the following story, Linda shares how she and her husband Kapp learned the benefits of mutual submission.

Stories from the Journey

 I am not a women's libber. I'm a sensitive person who hates conflict. So when I got married, I never thought submission would be a problem. But I had to learn that submission isn't just keeping the peace or being agreeable. It's deeper than that.

If Kapp and I differed in an area where I felt I had it all under control, I didn't consider his ideas or feelings. I just pushed his suggestions away. This was especially true in our shared leadership in a Christian ministry. I was sure my leadership style was right and his was wrong. Since I tend to be a perfectionist, I was determined to do my job the very best it could be done.

When the whole ministry team began to suffer from our competition, I knew I had to change. I started listening to Kapp's ideas and submitting some of my ideas to his leadership style. And guess what—his ideas worked, too! When I accepted his leadership, he began to show more leadership. The more I allowed Kapp to be the person God created him to be, the happier and more content I became. As my pride in him grew, his pride in me grew.

Linda, 30s, mother of one ■

164

Mutual submission affects our sexual relationship. Many people are amazed that basic principles for sex in marriage were written in the first century.

The husband should fulfill his marital duty to his wife, and likewise the wife to her husband. The wife's body does not belong to her alone but also to her husband. In the same way, the husband's body does not belong to him alone but also to his wife. Do not deprive each other except by mutual consent and for a time, so that you may devote yourselves to prayer. Then come together again so that Satan will not tempt you because of your lack of self-control.

1 Corinthians 7:3-5

God has given sex in marriage for our good and our enjoyment. The same responsibilities and privileges are given to the husband and the wife. There is no difference. Either partner can initiate sex. Each is to care for the needs of the other.

Any decision to abstain from sex is to be a mutual decision and for some good purpose. Sex is not to be withheld as a punishment or given as a reward.

A psychiatrist friend of ours is appalled at the number of couples he counsels who have not had sex for months or years. The wall between them has grown thicker and thicker, and expressions of tenderness have grown fainter and fainter. He tries to get them to begin to communicate with each other, which is the first step toward satisfying sex.

Today, Barbara and Nelson thrive on the joys of mutual submission and open communication. But it wasn't always like that. Barbara describes their painful struggle in the following story.

Stories from the Journey

During the years of Nelson's affair, I recognized my options.

I could become bitter, hateful, and full of self-pity by feeding on anger, pain, depression, and frustration. Or I could allow God to teach me what I needed to learn. I wanted to learn. So I set priority *one:* to obey and depend on Jesus Christ. Depend on his grace to face each day, to cope with new hurts, to emotionally support our two daughters still at home.

I had to admit I was part of the problem in our marriage and stop putting all the blame on my husband. Painful, honest self-examination focused my attention on changes God and I needed to work on.

First, instead of listing all the things Nelson shouldn't be doing, find ways to affirm him.

Second, stop demanding that God cure all our problems *now.*

Since Jesus loves our family and is in control, I can trust his patience and timing. Learning to wait quietly for God to work was like climbing a sand dune, three steps up and two steps back. Friends helped me wait. One reminded me that God wouldn't force Nelson against his own free will. It might take a long time for Jesus to get through to him. I needed to recognize that the painful verbal attacks Nelson hurled at me might be a smoke screen for his own feelings.

Third, keep daily appointments with God. Find promises to claim. Memorize verses on patience and waiting. Replace panic with prayer.

Five years is a long time to hang on. But as my confidence in God grew, Nelson began to notice changes in me. Healing of our relationship began and the other relationship ended. Learning to work together on our problem areas required new skills and patterns. I had to forgive, but what do I do with painful memories? I remembered that Jesus does not keep reminding me of my sins. They are gone forever. Isaiah 43:18-19 instructed me: "Forget the former things; do not dwell on the past. See, I am doing a new thing!" So when I say, "I forgive," never bring up the subject again.

Resist the temptation to relive the past pain.

How do you rebuild trust? One day at a time. One thoughtful word or deed, a changed attitude. Seeing my husband's openness to God and to me allows me to lay my worries at Jesus' feet.

Barbara, 50s, mother of five, grandmother of eight ■

Mutual submission also means helping each other in areas of weakness. We have learned to give and take advice from each other. As Jim leaves for work, he sometimes says with a smile but in a firm voice, "Don't try to do everything today." He knows my weakness for pushing to get to the bottom of the list. So he encourages me to take time to enjoy the daisies along the way.

Once he told me, "I have antisocial tendencies. Sometimes I'd rather have an evening to read than be with people." I assured him, "I enjoy just reading in the same room with you. But I think I can help you enjoy a party in our living room, too." We've helped balance each other. Lovingly he slows me down, and I introduce him to more people.

I am interdependent with many people: the car mechanic, the stove repair man, the doctor, the librarian, the garbage collector. They have skills I need, and they need my business. I am interdependent with friends and fellow Christians. We each need the acceptance, love, and talents of others. My interdependence with my husband shows in how we complement each other. Mutual submission in all these relationships is part of godliness.

Chapter Seventeen

No Matter How Hard
Things Get

Along the way, forgiveness

O n Tuesday morning before I started preparing for the
neighborhood Bible study, I remembered that I needed
to order a refill of my thyroid prescription. The last time it
was filled, the doctor ordered 300 tablets since it's something
I'll have to take all my life. But when I went to pick it up at
the drugstore, the pharmacist said I couldn't have 300. My
insurance company's rules stated that I could get only 100 at
a time. He could sell me 100 tablets three different times.
What a bother!

So a hundred days later, I made the routine call for a refill I
could pick up that afternoon. A few minutes later, the pharmacist called back to say that he couldn't refill the prescription. I would have to get a new one from my doctor.

Furious at the stupid complication, I stormed, "But the
doctor gave you an order for 300 the last time, and you only

sold me 100. You said I must buy them at three different times. Now you tell me my prescription time has elapsed."

"Mrs. Reapsome, I don't make the rules. The insurance company makes the rules. Are you saying I'm responsible?" he replied with calculated calmness.

"I knew something like this would happen. How can you need a new prescription from the doctor when you haven't filled the one he sent you? Now you're telling me I must call the doctor and asked him to send you another order," I protested in my most irate voice.

"Those are the rules I have to go by, but I don't make the rules," he repeated deliberately.

I slammed down the phone, called the doctor's office, waited for the nurse to be free to talk to me, told her my tale of woe, and asked for the doctor to authorize a new prescription. Then I tried to prepare for the Bible study. Concentration was impossible. I could think only about the endless red tape complicating my life. I was frustrated and powerless. And I had taken out my frustration on a person who was as bound by the red tape as I was.

As I sat there trying to cool off, the Holy Spirit pulled out of storage something I'd studied long before. "If you are offering your gift at the altar and there remember that your brother has something against you, leave your gift there in front of the altar. First go and be reconciled to your brother; then come and offer your gift" (Matthew 5:23-24).

"You mean I have to ask the pharmacist's forgiveness before I can go to Bible study?" I asked weakly. "Lord, you know I let my frustration turn to anger. I attacked a man who was just doing his job. I'm sorry for grieving you and for attacking him. With your help, I'll apologize to him today when I pick up the prescription. Please help me not to fall into this trap again."

What a relief to be forgiven by God and by the pharmacist! Mercy tasted sweet. Godliness is forgiving in the same way God forgives me—completely, never bringing up the matter again. I can never say that something is too terrible to forgive, since God has forgiven my proud rebellion against him and all the sins that have come from that. Because I've received mercy, I'm free to give mercy.

Stories from the Journey

 When we were missionaries in Iran, we invested in a Persian carpet as part of our family treasure. The rich colors and intricate design graced our living room and brought happy memories in every new location. An extended furlough meant putting our things in storage for several years. How do you store a Persian carpet to protect it from moths? The best protection is to keep it on the floor and sweep it regularly.

So we decided to leave it with a friend to use, but not the friends with cats.

"Enjoy the carpet while we're gone. But, please, don't roll it up and store it," we instructed Alice.

Friction soon arose between Alice and the friends who owned the cats. They were jealous of the lovely Persian carpet that Alice had instead of them. So Alice rolled up the carpet and stored it. "I won't let a carpet break our relationship," she declared.

When we returned to the Middle East, my husband went to retrieve our belongings from storage and our carpet from Alice.

I still remember his tone of voice as he tried to prepare me for the return of our "family treasure." He rolled it out across the floor, moth-eaten, full of holes. A destroyed treasure!

What do I do with the mixture of emotions choking me? How do I respond to this loss? What do I say to our children?

"Children, look at our carpet. Remember that jealousy destroyed our treasure. Jealousy will always destroy."

Rhoda, 50s, mother of five, grandmother of two ■

I've never had to forgive anything as painful as my friend Shirley has. Earlier, I told about her taking a foster daughter. Debbie enjoyed Shirley's love, her home, her gifts, opportunities for music lessons and for travel, all a single parent could give. But she completely rejected Shirley's moral and spiritual values. Debbie bragged about her promiscuous behavior. When she did marry, her children had to be taken by the court and put in foster care because of her neglect. That meant that Shirley was also cut off from contact with her four grandchildren. Now she sends gifts occasionally to the social worker who can deliver them to the children.

Shirley also took a foster son who followed a similar course. He traded his opportunity for education and his talents in art for a life marred by drugs, stealing, and homosexuality.

Shirley writes to me about her bitter pain, and she has given me permission to share some of her letters.

Stories from the Journey

 I think I'm a person with no lasting ability to love. I thought if one loved someone the love went on forever. I wonder if I am capable of that. I thought love endured no matter how hard things got. My feelings are changing toward my kids in a most bitter fashion.

I don't want to hear their voices. When I think of those poor, starving, sick, dirty babies, I think, "So love never dies?" I'm not sure but what my love has been murdered.

Could it be that love must sometimes be like the little woods creatures that go into underground burrows during hard, winter blizzards and come out again when the storm goes by? Otherwise they couldn't survive, you know. What a winter it is in my heart! I'll decide later whether to survive or turn to a fossil in the burrow. Fossils never have to learn to feel again.

In a later letter, she writes,

I reflected on your question, "Did God feel his love had been murdered?" First I thought, because his love, like himself, eternal, perhaps it is impossible for such a murder to occur. But assaults are certainly occurring constantly. Then I considered: "God is love," Jesus is God, and he was murdered, so in a sense love was murdered. So truly, God is no stranger to murder. It happened within the very Trinity. But a Resurrection was accomplished. This being true, one indeed has grounds for hope. This could get exciting yet.

I think I have proof that fossilization has not occurred. I talked with the social worker on the phone, trying to get news of baby Shelton. This was during the time that I was quite ill. Unknown to me, Mrs. Wilson became alarmed and contacted Debbie. She must have really raked her over the coals. Debbie called me sounding somewhat rebuked and chastened. But knowing Debbie, I arm myself with caution.

Oh, yes, Martha, I know I'm crazy! I'm just getting over a long illness, a winter storm is raging, and here I sit making plans for a trip into an emotionally charged situation to visit Debbie. I have heard that some animals are a little daft when they emerge from hibernation! ∎

Shirley fights self-pity and the urge to fossilize as she practices forgiveness. God gives her mercy and hope, and she comes out of hibernation and allows herself to love again.

Stories from the Journey

 My reflections on forgiveness began with a fractured friendship when both my friend and I were wrong. We sinned. We offered apologies. We extended forgiveness glibly and perhaps too quickly. Time and actions demonstrated what my friend should have said: "I'm trying to forgive you, but I still feel awfully hurt right now."

We both knew something was missing in the forgiveness process. We wanted to declare the other "forgiven" but somehow extract punishment.

This pain raised hard questions for me about forgiveness:

1. Do I believe that Jesus' cross is sufficient to forgive any sin, even this painful one?
2. Are there limits for restoring this relationship? If so, are they my limits or God's?
3. Doesn't forgiveness mean that we give up any desire to punish or humiliate one another?
4. Can't we still worship together?

The conflict between my friend and me remains unresolved. Like other relationship problems, this one has no tidy conclusion. I know God reads our thoughts, words, and actions accurately. I deeply appreciate Jesus' death to forgive and cover my sin, never remembering it against me again. May my friend and I someday be able to extend the "divine coverup" to each other.

Sue, 30s, mother of two ■

Joseph in the Old Testament is an example to all the Shirleys of this world who resist bitterness. He had been sold as a slave by his own brothers. Later he became a ruler in Egypt, in charge of famine relief. When his brothers came to buy food, they didn't recognize Joseph as the man who sold them food rather than let them starve.

After the famine, Joseph finally revealed his identity to them. They feared for their lives, but Joseph told them, "Don't be afraid. . . . You intended to harm me, but God intended it for good" (Genesis 50:19-20).

How did Joseph get that perspective? He didn't nurse the memory of their cruelty. He couldn't keep the memories from coming to his mind, but he didn't hold them, cherish the hurt, and relive each painful moment. He said, "God has made me forget all my trouble and all my father's household" (Genesis 41:51). Joseph forgave his brothers and then allowed God to erase the memories.

As my mother used to say, "You can't keep the birds from flying over your head, but you can keep them from building a nest in your hair." Instead of thinking over past injustice and pain, I need to think about what is true, pure, and lovely.

When I spoke to a women's seminar about the need to forget, I was amazed at the number of people who spoke to me afterward about Joseph's statement. They hadn't considered the possibility that God could help them forget wrongs and injustices: wrongs between mother and daughter, between sisters, between daughter-in-law and mother-in-law, between members of the church. But they saw that nourishing the painful experience was destroying them.

One woman who models forgiveness is Millicent Lindo. In the 1950s, Millicent and her husband, Lloyd, came from Jamaica to Wheaton College. Lloyd planned to complete a degree and return to Jamaica as a pastor. The college provided a list of addresses for possible apartments. As they drove from place to place, Lloyd and Millicent went to the door. No one had a vacancy for a black family. Eventually, someone at the college located a black family who made room for them.

When Millicent became pregnant, she searched for a doctor. One was recommended in a neighboring community. She sat in the waiting room, conspicuous as the only black in the roomful of pregnant women. After being kept waiting for hours, the doctor informed her that he wasn't taking any new patients. Humiliated and angry, she left.

When Lloyd and Millicent completed their studies, the Conservative Baptist denomination asked them to consider pastoring a black church in Chicago. They agreed to stay three years before returning to Jamaica. Twenty-four years later, they are still at Keystone Baptist Church. Lloyd teaches practical application of the Bible to the congregation: bitterness destroys the person who harbors it; channel anger against injustice into action to change the wrong.

One such action has been opening the Westside Holistic Family Center, which provides tutoring, home health courses, job placement, counseling, a parent drop-in center, and other services. Local schools refer families to this center, where Millicent directs the staff of competent counselors.

Each time I visit Keystone Baptist Church, I admire the graciousness of the Lindos and the congregation. They aren't allowing bitterness to destroy them. They have learned to forgive as they are forgiven along the path to godliness.

Chapter Eighteen

God's Refining Business

Along the way, suffering

s I left the house Tuesday morning to visit two friends, I
noticed the perfect summer sky, that marvelous Colorado blue with white fluffy clouds. A pleasant breeze was
blowing, and there was very little humidity. I had the whole
day to spend as I liked. Jim wouldn't be back from a meeting
in Atlanta until late afternoon. Sara was at church camp as a
counselor all week. John was at Pioneer Camp in Ontario,
Canada, where he had finished a month of leadership training
and had just been made a junior counselor.

When I returned to the house that afternoon, I was surprised to see Jim and two pastors from Calvary Church sitting
on the side porch with their chairs pulled together in a tight
circle. *What great plans are the three of them cooking up?* I
wondered in happy anticipation.

As I parked in front of the garage and started to take my
packages out of the car, Jim came to meet me. One look at his

179

face told me tragedy had struck. *It must be something about his mother,* I quickly told myself. Nothing could have prepared me for what came.

"John is with Jesus," he sobbed in my ear as he drew me close.

I still remember insisting, "No! No! You're wrong, it can't be." I still feel my sunglasses cutting into my face as Jim held me and repeated the truth until I stopped protesting.

Dazed and numb, we sat on the porch while Pastor Chrichton gave me the sketchy details. The camp director had been trying to call us since about 9:30. That was just a few minutes after I had left the house. When there was no answer, he called the church to tell the pastor that they had "a probable drowning." He asked the pastor to try to find us, and the pastor had continued to call all day until Jim returned, shortly before I did.

We moved into the house so that Jim could make the dreaded confirming call to the camp director. The camp director reported that John's body had been found. He was still trying to piece together what had happened. Monday had been a day off for John and three other counselors. They had gone into town to the Laundromat and returned to a cottage across the lake owned by one counselor's family. The family had given permission for them to spend the night there.

They awoke Tuesday morning, not sure what time it was. John was due to be on duty at his tent when the boys got up, and he didn't want to be late. Hurriedly, he stored his gear in the canoe for the short trip across the lake on that calm morning. He was a canoeing instructor. There was no reason for him not to go. But he didn't feel well. Returning to the cabin, he rested his head on the table for a few minutes. His friends tried, to no avail, to persuade him not to go. Being a counselor and being there on time were more important than how he felt.

Eric walked out to the canoe with John to see him off. Then he went back to clean up the cabin. A minute or two later, he looked out the window and saw only an empty canoe bobbing in the water. John had disappeared. Across the lake at camp, one of the counselors thought he saw someone swimming toward an empty canoe and wondered what was happening.

For hours the camp and the police tried to put the stories together and to find the body. Late in the afternoon, a police diver saw John's hand, the only light spot on the black, muddy lake bottom. John's jeans and navy windbreaker blended so the diver would never have seen them.

The coroner needed our permission to do an autopsy. Who did we want to contact to receive the body? What instructions did we want to give them? Like robots, we heard the questions and gave mechanical answers.

Friends from the Congregational Bible Church, where Jim was pastor, came to sit and cry with us. Pastor Crichton had called them earlier when he was trying to find us. They had waited all day in suspense, hoping and praying that the report was a mistake. Not being able to wait any longer, they came and knew by one look at us that the worst was true.

Jim poured out his bewilderment and fears about an unusual thing that had happened to him the previous night. Three times someone rang his motel room by mistake. After being awakened the third time, he thought maybe God was telling him to pray for his family. For some time he lay there praying for each of us by name. How did that fit in with what had happened to John?

Should I have walked the floor and prayed all night? Would that have saved John from drowning? were the unspoken questions I read in his eyes and heard from his heart.

The agony in his voice tore me apart. I couldn't believe that God would ask Jim to bear this grief in addition to all he had already had. To be widowed with two small children was enough for any man to suffer. How could God allow this, too?

Helping us do what had to be done, one of the pastors called a funeral director to come to the house. After we discussed the arrangements with him, we took the tragic news to our daughter, Sara, and then to Jim's mother.

Finally, we went home and went to bed. I slept very little, but sleep was better than waking. Each time I awoke, for an instant I thought, *It was a bad dream! John isn't dead. I just dreamed it.* Then the horror washed over me again.

The second night when I couldn't sleep, I sat in the rocker in the dark living room. "God, are you good? Are you in control? If you have lost control of the world, then I don't want to live. I can't live in a world you don't control. If you aren't good, I want to die," I cried desperately. I felt as vulnerable as if I were standing naked before a gaping universe.

In the silent darkness, a calm crept over me, and I began to remember. It was as though God was saying, "Do you remember the time when John was two and had the croup? The vaporizer broke and he stopped breathing, but you found him in time. You sat with him in the bathroom with the steaming shower running until the doctor arrived.

"Remember when he was four and he careened down the hill on his tricycle toward the intersection? The tricycle upset on the grass before it came to the street. I was merciful then.

"Remember when he was six and had rheumatoid arthritis? He recovered with no permanent damage. I was merciful then.

"Remember when he was eight and had pneumonia? He spent a month in the hospital because he didn't respond to the first medicine. I was merciful to him then.

"Remember the hunting accident when he was almost shot, and the canoeing trip when he held on to the rocks for hours? I delivered him then.

"Couldn't I have delivered him last Tuesday in the lake if that had been merciful?"

"Yes, Lord, I know you could have delivered him. Thank you for reminding me of all those times you were watching and caring for John in your mercy," I sobbed in agony. "But, oh God, I miss him so much! Lord, I do believe, help my unbelief," I pleaded as a helpless child.

The week wore on. Family and friends arrived. We had the private family viewing. We received John's things from camp. But it was the memorial service I was most concerned about. All week I wondered how I could get through the service on Sunday afternoon. Years ago I had attended the memorial service for Joe and Mary Lou Bayly's son Joey. I had been a basket case; I couldn't sing or pray or even hear the Scripture read. I couldn't speak to them except to whisper, "I'm sorry." Now I was going to my son's service.

Jim and Sara and I received friends in the church vestibule before they were seated in the sanctuary. The church organist played for two hours as friends came and waited for the service to begin. In front of the sanctuary was John's casket. When we had to choose the casket, we both knew a beautifully finished oak one was right for John. It represented his love of nature and a promise we were claiming,

> *They will be called oaks of*
> *righteousness,*
> *a planting of the LORD*
> *for the display of his splendor.*
>
> Isaiah 61:3

When it was time for us to be ushered down the aisle to the second row, I couldn't believe my calmness. I wasn't crying, and I was aware of the people around me. I sang every hymn. I heard every Scripture reading, every prayer, the words of comfort, and the sermon.

Later as I told a friend about this mystery, that I could sing at John's funeral but not at Joey's, she said, "It's because God gives grace and comfort to those who need it. Behind you were hundreds of us praying for you through our tears." What a precious revelation to my grieving heart.

At the grave side, blinded by tears, I heard the words:

> *Death has been swallowed up*
> *in victory.*

Where, O death, is your victory?
Where, O death, is your sting?

1 Corinthians 15:54-55

I knew this wasn't the end. John Reapsome was not in the ground. His body was there to await the victory of resurrection, but John was in the presence of God, full of joy and pleasures forevermore.

We chose the confident words from Psalm 16:11 to be engraved on John's memorial stone: "In thy presence there is fulness of joy, in thy right hand are pleasures for evermore" (RSV).

I learned many lessons from this grief. That God gives grace to those who need it is a big one. That grief is slow is another. I discovered that the process can't be hurried. For hours I sat in the back yard reading the Bible and writing in my prayer journal.

Meditating on Isaiah 40, I saw that the almighty God comes to me and my hurting family as tenderly as a loving shepherd.

God cares for all the stars of the universe, calling them by name. Not one is ever missing. If God knows by name every inanimate star, which is not even a creature made in his image or redeemed by his Son, surely God knows John by his name. John isn't missing. He's in God's presence.

God didn't grow faint or weary or fall asleep on August 2. He was and is the Creator, the everlasting God, all-powerful, all-wise, all-loving when he called John by name and took his hand.

Second Corinthians was a more appropriate book to be reading that summer than I could have guessed when I began it. The word *weakness* jumped out of every page. We can only boast of things that show our weakness (11:30). God's power is perfected in weakness (12:9). Jesus "was crucified in weakness, yet he lives by God's power" (13:4)! So John died in weakness but lives by God's power. My weakness really qualified me for the help I needed from God.

Like the hurt little girl who used to sit in my Daddy's lap, I sat in God's lap, letting him comfort me. For months I was sure I'd never sing again. Then one day I heard myself singing. *So that's why God is called the Father of compassion and the God of all comfort,* I thought.

Another evidence that grief is slow would come just when I'd think I was in control and some little thing would stab me again. One day in the grocery store, I suddenly realized I was buying fruit in multiples of four—four pears, eight oranges. But there weren't four in my family any longer. Tears flowed, and I wanted to scream. For a minute I thought I'd have to leave my cart and run out of the store.

Another day I was returning from a Bible study just as the high school was letting out. As I turned the corner, there were two boys from John's class, tall, straight, handsome, smiling. Suddenly, the pain stabbed into my heart with gruesome force. My son would never stand on the corner joking with his friends again. I could no longer anticipate his cheerful "Hi!" as he came in the door. The finality almost drove me off the road.

But I also learned that it was wise to avoid situations I knew would be too hard. One of the neighbors in the Bible study lives on the hill overlooking the cemetery where John is buried. When we met at her house, I was careful to sit with my back to the window so I wouldn't see his grave. I also stopped sitting on the center aisle of the church. Several Sundays when I struggled to control my tears, I thought I might have to leave the service. Just sitting on the outside aisle and farther back would make my exit less noticeable.

In March, seven months after John's death, I became depressed in a way I had never been before. I wondered if I was normal. After seven months of grief, why was this happening to me? During that time, Joe Bayly came to visit. Joe and Mary Lou have survived the death of three sons. They had been a great help to us already. I confided in Joe about my depression and asked if he thought it was normal.

His reply both stunned and comforted me. "For years I've been depressed at Christmas. It was Christmas night that Joey had his sledding accident."

I wasn't glad my friend was depressed at Christmas. But he reassured me I wasn't the only Christian contending with depression.

I learned I had to accept my feelings and talk honestly about them. I didn't need anyone to say, "You shouldn't feel that way." What I needed was someone who would accept me and my feelings. Jim did that for me. I could voice my doubts about God's goodness and power to Jim, knowing he wouldn't be destroyed by them, nor would he reject or criticize me.

Holding me tenderly, more sure than I that we would survive this flood, he'd confirm what I knew deep inside, "We have to keep remembering what we know about the character of God."

Then I'd remind myself again of all the years of evidence I had that God can be trusted. I remembered the times God had spared John. I walked through my past, reliving God's goodness to me, my family, and my friends. My hungry soul feasted on every story I knew of God's faithfulness to people I knew and to those I had read about.

I also learned that some books could help me, but others couldn't. *Mourning Song* by Joyce Landorf was a great help in understanding grief. *Heaven* by Joseph Bayly enlarged my hope for heaven and resurrection. *Figures of the True* by Amy Carmichael comforted me with its wise lessons drawn from reflecting on a photograph.

The "figure of the true" that best described how I saw myself is the picture of a bare bush in winter with its branches casting shadows on the snow.

You were like a leafy bush, and many little things came to you for shelter. You were not great or important, but you could help those little things. And it was the joy of your life to help them.

Now you cannot do anything at all. Some desolation, illness, poverty, or something that you cannot talk about, has overwhelmed you, and all your green leaves have gone. So you cannot shelter even the least little bird; you are like this bush with its bare twigs, no use to anyone—that is what you think.

But look again at this bush. Look at the delicate tracery of lines on the snow. The sun is shining behind the bush, and so every little twig is helping to make something that is very beautiful. Perhaps other eyes, that you do not see, are looking on it too, wondering at what can be made of sun and snow and poor bare twigs. And the Spring will come again, for after Winter there is always Spring.

When will the Spring come? When will your bush be green again? When will the little birds you love come back to you? I do not know. Only I know that Sun and Snow are working together for good; and the day will come when the very memory of helplessness to help, and bareness, and poverty and loneliness will pass as a dream of the night; and all that seemed lost will be restored.

Now in the multitude of the sorrows that you have in your heart, let these comforts refresh your soul. They will not fail you for He will not fail you who is the God of the Sun and of the Snow. (Amy Carmichael, *Figures of the True)*

I also learned from our friends how to help a grieving friend. I learned not to say, "Is there something I can do for you?" The answer would probably be no. But a specific offer tells what I can and want to do and how much time I can offer.

Betty offered to wash all of John's clothes. Blanche took the baskets of ripe pears, canning jars, and sugar and returned them canned. Nancy came for my grocery list to do my shopping when she did hers. Janet "house sat" when we had to go to the funeral home and to see Sara.

Friends brought pots of soup, meat loaves, cakes, salads. The neighborhood Bible study group served lunch to all the family on Saturday. The women of the church served Saturday night supper. Neighbors and friends served Sunday dinner before the funeral. They made decisions and took care of details when I couldn't think about them. The morning after the funeral, Elaine offered to be my "maid" for the day.

I learned some things about praying for grieving friends. If the death is sudden, as John's was, I pray for their first waking moments. I remember the horror of realizing all over again that it wasn't a bad dream but a reality.

I've learned to use the prayer that my friend Grace prayed for me: "Lord, remind her today of what she knows about you and your promises."

Jane taught me to give a treasured memory to a grieving friend. From her younger son, David, Jane learned something about John that only David knew.

"Now nobody will shoot baskets with me," David sobbed as he told about John's staying at the school yard to play basketball with him after the high-school fellows left. They wouldn't let David play because he was too little.

"John was my friend, and I miss him." David's words gave me a precious picture of my son that no one else could give.

I was surprised to learn that it helps to talk about the one who is gone. In the months after John's death, I appreciated the friends who would ask me things about John or mention him in our conversation. They weren't reminding me of someone I had forgotten or reviving a hurt. We were remembering together someone we both loved.

I couldn't talk about John and my pain with everyone. It was too heavy. But I'm thankful for the friends who would look me in the eye and say, "How are you this week?" I knew they wanted to know how I was coping. I could say, "I'm doing all right." Or, "It was a hard week. I really need your prayers." And I knew they prayed. Sometimes a card or note would come to say they cared. Some weeks I just felt the weight lift. They never quoted Romans 8:28 to me. I didn't need to be told that God was working everything, even grief, for good. I just needed to know that someone cared enough to share my pain.

I saw that God doesn't build a fence around his children to protect us from the suffering common to all humanity. It is clear from the Bible and from the lives of Christians in every generation that God uses suffering in some form in the life of every believer.

Stories from the Journey

 Our daughter, Amy, chose the wild and rebellious kids in the high school for friends. Dave, her steady boyfriend, lived in a home where teenage drinking and sexual immorality were accepted.

The more she rebelled against our Christian standards, the more I talked, pushed, and criticized. No discipline worked, my kind or my husband's.

Our marriage suffered as we fought Amy and each other. In desperation I moved closer to Jesus, but my husband moved away. I loved Amy unconditionally, though I hated her lifestyle.

Nelson's anger mushroomed as he lost control of this daughter who should obey and respect him. She fought for independence and identity. He fought to keep a tight rein on her. They pulled in opposite directions. I stood in the middle trying to be a peacemaker for both sides.

When I thought tensions couldn't get worse, Amy announced she was pregnant. I identified with the book title *Where Does a Mother Go to Resign?* I could only go to Jesus, not to resign, but to cry, scream, pray, wait, listen. Gradually, comfort and promises kindled hope. I entrusted

Amy and her unborn child into Jesus' hands, trusting him to bring good out of a bad situation.

Jesus brought Amy back to himself. With the help of The House of His Creation, a home for single pregnant girls, Amy gave birth to a healthy daughter. The daughter we thought we had lost came home to a thankful family. As our relationship healed, Amy matured spiritually and emotionally. A few years later, God brought Nick into her life, a loving, godly husband. The miracles God worked in Amy encouraged me to trust him to heal my marriage, which he has done, and to trust him to bring good out of current impossible situations.

Barbara, 50s, mother of five, grandmother of eight ■

Along the path to godliness, there may be disease, birth defects, unemployment, accidents, abuse, rejection, poverty, persecution, injustice, war, famine, floods, fire, a son in prison, a daughter institutionalized with mental illness. In these tests of faith that suffering brings, we're asked to endure, stay on the path, and keep trusting God. The end won't be our destruction, but will be our good and our godliness.

The list of the faithful in the Hebrews 11 Hall of Fame includes those who "through faith . . . shut the mouths of lions, quenched the fury of the flames, and escaped the edge of the sword" (verses 33-34) and those who "were tortured . . . Some faced jeers and flogging . . . They were stoned; they were sawed in two; they were put to death by the sword" (verses 35-37). "These were all commended for their faith" (verse 39).

In the years since I first wrote this book, suffering of a special nature has grown in the awareness of Christians and non-Christians alike: the sexual abuse of children. Recently this issue has seared my heart like a branding iron. While we are all victims of financial setbacks, dashed dreams, and health problems, it is difficult to include childhood sexual abuse as "par for the course"; what happens to children in these situations is simply evil, and it breaks the heart of God.

Five of my friends, men and women, faced the unspeakable—abuse by people they trusted, betrayal by people who should have protected them.

Why do I know five brave survivors working through the long, painful healing process? Perhaps God assigned me to their support teams to learn how a friend can help a survivor.

They recite a litany of losses. Losses of innocence, trusted relationships, a sense of belonging, self esteem, security, permission to have and express needs. In return they received fear, anxiety, worthlessness, rejection, inadequacy before God and people, anger against themselves, despair, and a sense of shame. They feel a sense of shame, thinking *I am evil* rather than the common sense of guilt, *I did evil*.

Abuse taught them four messages: "Don't tell"; "Don't trust"; "Don't feel"; "Don't say no to me." To survive they buried their traumatic memories. When in danger, they shut down feelings until later, when the needed time, energy, and support made it safe to feel the pain.

After suppressing reality for years, they are facing buried memories and beginning the slow process of grief. Realizing you were never loved for yourself and protected by your parents pushes one to despair. Anger long denied must be felt, owned, and dealt with. Weeping and grieving are essential parts of healing.

"My counselor says that a survivor's primary need is a sense of belonging," explained Wendy. "Someone who has been abandoned by her family feels *alone!* I'm learning that the people of integrity in the church are my family. I don't have to work this through alone. Rachel has made me feel that we are working on this healing process together. I'm not her 'ministry' or 'project.' We're equals, giving and receiving from each other. She dispells my fear that I'm not a person but an object to be used."

I've been on the primary support team of one of these friends. I could never understand why over the years Emily found it so hard to believe that I loved and respected her. Now that she realizes her parents emotionally abandoned her as a baby and then abused her for years, I marvel that she gave and accepted love at all.

As Mother's Day approached, I anticipated her sense of loss.

As a motherless child, sitting in church and listening to mothers being praised could only add to her grief. So that afternoon I called to tell her that I especially wanted her to know on Mother's Day that I love her.

Her note reinforced for me what Emily needed from me. "I just finished talking to you and feeling such joy, love, and gratitude. Your call meant so much to me today. I was over-whelmed with tiredness and sadness when you called. The Lord reached down through your call and made me know I'm loved and belong to you and a few others. It means so much to know you hear my pain, that you care and want to be part of its healing and are praying to that end. Thursday my counselor asked who I *knew* loved me without hesitation. You were the one person who came to my thoughts, for you have proved it again and again over many years—at least I'm that far in my process! I love you. And am so happy you want me to know I'm loved on Mother's Day!!!"

Because of the nature of childhood sexual abuse, most victims need more help than what I can offer in the scope of this book. However, I have included some general guidelines for recovery; they are listed in the Appendix at the end of this book. Included in this Appendix is a listing of helpful resources. If you or a friend has been sexually abused, I encourage you to seek help from a professional counselor—someone you can trust, someone trained in dealing with this specific issue.

God is in the refining business. If gold, which lasts only on earth, must be refined of all impurities to be of great value, is it surprising that our faith, far more precious to God than gold, requires refining? Even Jesus "learned obedience from what he suffered" (Hebrews 5:8). Jesus' resurrection and glory sprang from his suffering and death. With God, suffering can produce godliness.

Run with perseverance the race marked out for us. Let us fix our eyes on Jesus, the author and perfecter of our faith, who for the joy set before him endured the cross.... Consider him who endured such opposition from sinful men, so that you will not grow weary and lose heart. . . . God disciplines us for our good, that we may share in his holiness. No discipline seems pleasant at the time, but painful. Later on, however, it produces a harvest of righteousness and peace for those who have been trained by it.

Hebrews 12:1-3, 10-11

Chapter Nineteen

Intuition and the Holy Spirit

Along the way, listening

One Sunday morning as I sat in church enjoying the organ prelude and quieting myself for worship, I suddenly had an overwhelming urge to pray for my friend Holly. She and a missionary colleague live in a remote town in an Arab country. I hadn't heard from her in months, but that wasn't unusual. She and Carla befriend the Arab women, study the Bible with those who are interested, and help the small local church in any way they are asked.

I didn't know of any immediate crisis Holly might be facing, so I prayed for her basic needs: for her physical health and safety, for her personal walk with God, for her daily prayer and Bible study, for her friendships with women around her, for her wise use of time and energy, for the good sense to take a day off, for her relationship with Carla.

Then I turned my attention to the worship service, but I couldn't concentrate on the hymns, the Scripture reading, or the sermon. The urge to pray for Holly persisted. Throughout the service, I kept praying through every possible kind of need that came to mind. The prompting to pray continued for several days.

By Tuesday I decided I needed to write to her. Was there some crisis there? How should I pray? Eventually she answered my letter. Her partner, Carla, had been called home to care for an elderly parent, leaving Holly alone, the only American woman in that Arab town. Living as a single foreign woman in that culture was a very questionable thing to do. Isolation and loneliness gripped her. Doubts about herself and about God raged in her mind. Was she right to stay? Could God protect her and provide for all her needs under the circumstances?

She saw my letter as a reassurance that God hadn't forgotten her. God had even spoken to someone else about her. She could relax and not be afraid.

The whole experience both thrilled and frightened me. It was thrilling to know that the Holy Spirit could speak to me about someone else's need and that I could help even when I didn't know the details. It was frightening to think that I could have not listened, that I could have turned off the urging to pray.

Being transformed to the image of Jesus includes feeling what he feels and caring about what he cares about. I need to learn to listen to the various ways God speaks. That is an important part of godliness.

Stories from the Journey

 I'm struggling to learn to listen to God. I spent years in an authoritarian church that replaced Father, Son, and Holy Spirit with Father, Son, and Holy Bible. Counsel came only from older brothers or sisters. How awkward and uncomfortable to believe that God speaks to me and expects me to hear and obey.

I'm always looking for someone else, usually my husband, to make spiritual decisions for me. But God gave me a husband who sends me first to God and the Bible.

God accelerated my transition from deafness to hearing three times in the past year. First, with a call at work from Social Services. A social worker told me about Alex, a six-year-old of mixed race. His foster-care parents of three years were too old to adopt him. Their deteriorating health forced a move for Alex.

As I listened, my spirit was saying, "Yes, yes" while my head and my lips said, "No, I'm sorry. I've already talked to Sterling. Sometime in the future, we plan to take a mixed race child. But this isn't the right time."

"Yes, I will talk to my husband," I promised.

That evening I started telling Sterling about the call. Five minutes into the conversation, he exclaimed, "Let's go for it."

"What? But we decided that it's too soon," I protested.

"I know," he said, "But something in my spirit says this is from God."

Confirmation! The message in my heart matched the message in my husband's heart. We would obey. Though married less than a year and Sterling unemployed, we began the adoption process.

A year later Sterling enjoyed a promotion on the new job, and Alex filled our hearts and home with joy. We celebrated the day the adoption became final with his favorite Baker's Square pie at lunch and an afternoon in the park.

Second, working hard to get out of debt, we considered moving into a less expensive apartment. On a lark, one January day, we looked at the apartment a friend recommended. Fifteen miles closer to Sterling's job and Alex's school and four hundred dollars a month cheaper convinced us that this was God's place for us. But our obedience came harder this time. The idea of moving totally unsettled Alex. Every single day he got into trouble at school and at home. We were at our wits' end. Thank goodness February only had twenty-nine days this year, because after our move on March first, he settled down. On March fifth a pink slip suddenly announced that I was laid off! Had we not moved, our rent would have made it impossible to pay off our debts. God knew what was coming. A major lesson in listening and obeying.

The third lesson began as a "coincidence." I sent out numerous resumes to hospitals that might need a recreational therapist. One landed on the nurse manager's desk of a small psychiatric unit in a nearby hospital. She called with a vague offer. At the interview, we clicked with each other. But all she could offer was five hours per week.

I kept looking for full-time work but couldn't get her offer out of my mind. One morning while praying, I was sure

God was telling me to take the five hours. "But God, it'll
mess up my unemployment. It'll make it harder for me to
look for full-time work. But . . . but . . . but . . . O.K. I'll take
it."

Two days later, the manager called to say the occupational
therapist had quit. I could work as many hours as I wanted at
the same hourly contract wage, which literally doubled my
income from the previous full-time job! Today, I'm in my
fifth week of this "temporary" job, with hopes of a long-term
part-time position, just what I want.

As I learn to listen to God, I'm enjoying the promise: "If
you are willing and obedient, you will eat the best from the
land" (Isaiah 1:19).

Marti, 30s, mother of one ■

I've already mentioned some of the ways in which God
speaks to us—through nature, through the Bible, through
others, and through suffering. In addition to speaking through
these external voices, God speaks internally. He spoke through
the Holy Spirit in urging me to pray for Holly. He also speaks
to me through intuition.

Webster's Unabridged Dictionary defines *intuition* as "the
immediate knowing or learning of something without the
conscious use of reasoning; instantaneous apprehension." In
science, the arts, and business, breakthroughs have occurred
in the "eureka" moment. Suddenly, a person knows something not known before and not consciously reasoned out.
This hunch or revelation is one meaning of intuition.

For the Christian, this intuitive revelation may be indistin-
guishable from the promptings of the Holy Spirit. I'm not

sure I can always distinguish between them. But I'm not sure I need to make a distinction if I respond properly. Sometimes the idea flashes in my mind, *Call Joan and invite her to lunch.* Or, *Write to Beth.* When I've followed through on the impulse, I've been glad. Their responses confirm the rightness of the timing of my call or letter. The time spent somehow doesn't destroy anything that *has* to be done that day. I seem to be able to accomplish more in the remaining time than I normally do.

Stories from the Journey

 Aging is God's finishing school. We lose one thing after another. It is hard to give up our sight, hearing, walking, memory, independence, relationships, friends, usefulness, mobility. I'm more thankful than ever that I don't have to give up the flow of the Spirit through my life! My hearing is impaired, but I can hear the Lord more clearly.

Lois, 80s ■

I've sat in a meeting in which everything seemed congenial and aboveboard. But I realized that I was getting a knot in my stomach and my body was tensing up. I was not consciously, by my senses, picking up anything negative, but my body told me something else was going on besides words and ideas. I would be foolish to ignore what intuition tells me.

Learning to listen to God raises my sensitivity to the Holy Spirit and to intuition.

Sometimes a prompting or a hunch goes against reason. Lucy told me of such a prompting. She and her sister met at their grandmother's house for Thanksgiving. Lucy hadn't seen her sister Connie for some time, since Connie's marriage to a non-Christian. Lucy was eager to bridge the gap that had come between them.

"When Connie and I were alone in Grandmother's kitchen for a few minutes, I felt the urge to ask her how she was doing. But it seemed an intrusive question when I was trying to rebuild our friendship," Lucy told me.

"Also, the timing was all wrong. No one was supposed to be in the kitchen but the servants. We could be interrupted and ordered out at any minute," she continued.

"As I was thinking of all the reasons not to ask Connie, 'How are you doing?' I remembered hearing a speaker say, 'God may say something only once.'

"So right there, in the wrong place and at the wrong time, I said what seemed like the wrong thing."

In response to Lucy's questions, the tragic details of Connie's last few months came tumbling out. Connie was on the verge of alcoholism; she was seeing a man and considering having an affair with him; the previous week she had tried to commit suicide.

Lucy's question came when Connie was ready, although the timing didn't make any sense to Lucy. In the conversations that followed during the weekend, Connie faced her sin and brought her needs to God. As Lucy reminded her of God's promises and faithfulness, Connie was reconciled to God and eventually to her husband.

When I get a persistent urge to do something that doesn't make sense to do or to do now, I ask myself some questions: Does it violate anything in the Bible? Does it hurt anyone? Does it honor God or feed my ego?

The promptings from the Holy Spirit are always right, but intuition isn't infallible. It needs evidence to confirm it. I don't have to apologize for saying, "I know this, but I don't know how I know it." But I need to look for the confirmation of that insight.

Two different times in different places, I've known I was going to be asked to be the chairman of the committee to plan a women's retreat. But I don't know how I knew it. When the call came, I heard it as God's confirmation that I should accept the responsibility.

In the spring of 1977, I knew God was giving me the job of being the speaker at the fall meeting for the neighborhood Bible studies in Lancaster. The committee chose the theme "Learning to Listen: To God, to Your Neighbor." Over the summer I read and thought about the theme and began to form an outline for the talk. Then August second came with the news of John's drowning.

I thought, *Surely I've misunderstood. Surely God isn't asking me to speak publicly just a month after my son's funeral, and certainly not about listening to God.*

But there was no escaping the inner conviction that this was exactly what God wanted. God had not been taken by surprise by John's death. He knew the timing from the beginning. God knew the lessons I would learn about listening that needed to be shared with that audience.

Some research into temperament types indicates that people have two distinct and sharply contrasting ways of perceiving information. Usually an individual is the *sensing type* or the *intuitive type. (Intuitive* here has to do not with the hunch or revelation I just described, but with a way of seeing reality. The sensing type perceives by using the five senses. The intuitive type perceives by scanning, glancing, and incorporating ideas or associations from the unconscious. The sensing type gets facts, uses logic, and accumulates details. The intuitive type picks up the big picture, gets an impression, and sees the possibilities. The sensing type focuses on the present. The intuitive type focuses on the future, drawing facts from the past that apply.

Recognizing these differences helps me understand why I have trouble "hearing" some people. When I served on a committee with Carol, I listened to her big ideas, her dreams of conquering all the problems of the world. As a sensing type, I thought, *She isn't being realistic. We can't tackle four major projects this month. We don't have the time or the money to do what she's talking about.*

But Carol, the intuitive type, said, "You aren't seeing the big picture. Remember how God has worked in the past. We can depend on his providing what we need for this next venture. We have to be willing to take risks. That's living by faith."

Apparently, we are born capable of both ways of perceiving. But from early childhood, most of us develop a preference for one and allow the other to go undeveloped. On the Myers-Briggs Type Indicator, a test widely used for identifying temperament types, I score much higher in sensing than in intuition. Jim scores higher in intuition. Women are usually credited with intuition and men have "hunches," but research shows intuition isn't restricted to women. *(Please Understand*

Me, by David Keirsey and Marilyn Bates, gives the basic information and some important applications of the temperament types.)

Jim and I have often benefited by comparing our responses to conversations or new situations. Sometimes I've come away from a meeting saying, "I was very uncomfortable there. I can't tell you why, but I don't think everything is as it appears." Other times Jim is the one who feels cautious and says, "Let's wait and watch in this relationship." Later something happens to verify our caution.

Because I want to develop all the facilities God gives me for hearing him, I need to develop the intuitive way of perceiving and learn to listen to intuitive people. Taking risks, considering unfamiliar ideas, not dismissing them as foolish and impractical, and leaving the door open to new possibilities are things I need to practice.

Stories from the Journey

 When we had a Christmas tree farm, I gave a copy of *The Cross and the Switchblade,* by David Wilkerson, to everyone who bought and dug a tree. One day I found a letter pushed under our door. It was from a woman who had bought a tree. "When I saw the book you gave me, I thought it was some religious junk. But when my older daughter read it, Jesus changed her life. Now my other daughter and I have read it and enjoy forgiveness through Jesus."

Esther Mae, 80s, mother of five, grandmother of eleven ■

If Carol, the intuitive type, is to develop sensing skills, she needs to practice gathering specific facts that lead her to her conclusions, finishing her sentences, and completing one idea before going to another.

I'm trying to develop both sensing and intuitive ways of listening to God. Jesus used both facts and feelings, logic and imagination, details and the big picture. To be more like him, I want to learn to "hear" both.

Chapter Twenty

Good or Better?

Along the way, choosing values

In 1984, cosmetic magnate Estee Lauder—who made Clinique, Aramis, and White Linen household words— was listed among a group of women most admired by other American women.

Estee Lauder calls her Creme Pack and Youth Dew "jars of hope." She tells women: "Time is not on your side, but I am." And she adds, "You have to feel rich to have the security that your face looks finished. You can have beautiful jewels and beautiful clothes, but your face must glow." Enough women have believed her to make her one of the four hundred richest Americans, with personal assets of $233 million.

Estee Lauder's success represents the high value our culture places on eternal youth and outward beauty. Although youth and a pretty face aren't evil, they aren't high on God's list of values, either.

You may have realized that all through this book I've been talking about values—God's values versus those of society. We choose between them many times a day. Sometimes we're aware that we're making a choice; other times it just happens, and later we realize that we bought a lie.

The media constantly remind us of society's values. To remember God's values, we have to take the initiative. The Longenecker family gave me one clue for doing that. I admired their children's behavior and the confidence the parents placed in them. One evening when the children were playing in the basement while we adults talked in the living room, their youngest came up to complain about something the others were doing. Her mother replied, "I'm sure you children are wise enough to work that out."

And they did. I asked Rhoda her secret.

She replied, "When our first son was a baby, we heard a psychiatrist say that parents should read parts of the book of Proverbs to their children every day. Though he wasn't speaking as a Christian, he saw that by the time a child is three years old, he could begin to distinguish between wise and foolish behavior.

"We've done that with the children, reading a few proverbs every day and talking about them. Now that they are old enough, we're trying to memorize the book of Proverbs. I try not to label their behavior 'good or bad' but 'wise or foolish.'"

By the time I learned this from Rhoda, Sara and John were almost teenagers, but we began reading a chapter of Proverbs nightly. Each of the four of us had to pick out two proverbs that impressed us and tell why. Peer pressure issues came up in almost every chapter, as did the value of integrity and the consequences of wise and foolish choices.

I wasn't surprised to read that along with his other Bible study, Billy Graham reads a chapter of Proverbs each day of the month, which is convenient since there are thirty-one chapters. I make it a habit to read the book one month each year.

In chapter seven you met Ellen, who reaped the benefits of her gentle response to her husband, Pete. In the following story she tells how she chose to put people above comfort and things.

Stories from the Journey

Three children under five years old kept me super busy. I was happy being a wife, mother, and homemaker. But our marriage wasn't at all like the stories in the Grace Livingston Hill books. I wasn't the most patient mother, but surely my priorities were in order. My home was immaculate and the children well behaved, and we went to church every Sunday. What more could a woman want?

Our social life centered around certain friends, so I wanted the same "things" they had. The only trouble was, my husband didn't. They all had new homes; we had an older house. They hired workmen to repair or remodel; we did everything ourselves as we could afford it. They drove new cars; ours was old, but paid for. Their kids' clothes had designer labels. Our kids wore hand-me-downs except for what I made. The contrasts robbed me of my happiness.

Then we bought a really *old* house, built in 1810. At least it had electricity and indoor plumbing. We put in all of the second-hand things—now lovingly called antiques—that we had bought at auctions over the years. Pete thrived on planting an orchard, a vineyard, and a garden that would make the Green Giant jealous. I worked at creating one spot of order and beauty in spite of sawdust, plaster dust, floor sanding, windows that wouldn't open, and doors that wouldn't shut.

As winter came, Pete brooded over an apple tree that wouldn't bear fruit. It was a Red Delicious, and we were most anxious for fruit. It got a few blossoms each spring, but never an apple.

Then he heard about a strange procedure called "ringing the tree." He took a sharp knife and cut the bark around the base of the tree, being careful not to cut deep enough to wound the tree's lifeline, just deep enough to get the tree's attention.

That's what God needed to do to me. Get my attention. He cut deeply into my life through three teenagers, two of them rebellious sons; through lessons in submission in this unequally yoked marriage; and through discontent with what I had and with what I could accomplish.

It was as though God said, "Ellen, I want a closer relationship with you. It is time to grow. Let me show you real joy. You can bear the fruit of the Spirit. Walk with me."

Pete hadn't been sure about the drastic measure of ringing his apple tree. So he had cut only halfway around the trunk. To our surprise, we got apples on that half of the tree. The next winter, Pete got the attention of the other half of that apple tree.

God is producing the fruit of the Spirit since he got my attention. But I anticipate a greater harvest as I choose his values over mine.

Ellen, 50s, mother of three, grandmother of five ■

Seeing God's values in comparison with society's values helps us to check ourselves. Each society creates its own value system, but God will judge all societies by his values. So we ask, "How does this idea compare with what the Bible says? How does it match with God's character?"

The following list of values from the Bible is not exhaustive, but it gives us enough to work on.

1. *Inner beauty is better than outer beauty.* The godly woman praised in Proverbs 31 cared well for her wardrobe, but she was remembered for her character. Perhaps you've known a beautiful woman like Christine, who spends lots of time and money on her clothes and grooming to perfect a stunning image, but the contrast of her demanding manner and critical remarks cancels the impression she wants to make.

2. *Wisdom and integrity are better than security and wealth.* The company for which Carl was controller decided on a new policy that was unethical. He had to make a choice. As a Christian, he could not participate in something he knew was dishonest, but he had a mortgage, a wife, and five children. When Carl said that he could not be a party to the new policy, the president replied, "Then your God can take care of you somewhere else. You are finished here."

Unemployment was frightening, but God did take care of Carl and his family. They depended on God as their basic security, and he honored their integrity.

In chapters fourteen, fifteen, and seventeen you met Shirley as she learned to confront, to forgive, and to give herself permission to need other people. In the following story, she recounts God's more recent lesson that caring is better than comfort.

Stories from the Journey

 Retiring from teaching freed me to experiment with living in a drier climate. New Mexico's beauty, desert vegetation, unusual rocks, and mild winters tempted me to move. But my comfortable little house—filled with memories and mementos from hundreds of second graders, next door to my church, in the town where I knew everyone by name—pulled me back like a bungee cord.

On my first Sunday back in church, I noticed a tall, gray-haired man walking with a white cane. A friend introduced me to Henry, the local piano tuner, who had recently joined the church. Each Sunday this blind man managed to locate me in the congregation. Sometimes he sat down beside me; other times he'd find me chatting with friends after the service.

"Henry has been asking lots of questions about this retired teacher who just came back from New Mexico," a friend confided to me.

Less than two years later, we stood before our family and friends in the pastor's living room to be married. Some people wondered how this unlikely gray-haired pair could be acting like two lovesick teenagers. Since my little house was in better condition than his, Henry moved from town into our rural community.

As winter storms darkened the sky, Henry's hostile mood darkened our home. After an angry outburst, Henry began to explain his frustration. Living in a small town with no sidewalks where he could get out on his own and "cane walk" was weighing on him far more oppressively than he had expected. He felt trapped. "It's not your fault. I got myself into this. I thought I could handle it, but I find I can't. I will have to learn to cope until we can afford a house in town. Delaying our marriage wouldn't have been the answer. We've got too much that is good going for us that I really wouldn't have wanted to miss."

My husband needed to move from the safe, comfortable home I had created for myself over the years. He needed clutter-free space, nothing extra to bump into, no knick-knacks to upset. My shelves and shelves of books, collectables, and mementos from students, which gave a homey touch for me, complicated life for the man I loved. With mixed feelings I prepared for a garage sale as the first step in putting Henry before the house and things I cherished.

We found the ideal house in town, where Henry could "cane walk" all over; walk to work, to the grocery, to the bank. How good for his back and for his independence. In the shop attached to the house, he could rebuild pianos and make brooms.

I'm not nearly as lonesome for the old place as I expected to be. This place feels more and more like home. It's great to see Henry so content. This place fits him like a glove. It is a lovely house, good floor plan, and storage space. Henry senses it's a lovely house even though he can't see it.

He brooded over the condition of our old couch, the one the cat autographed with such flourish. We decided to celebrate Christmas and our first anniversary with a new couch. But Henry couldn't wait till December. "I want you to have it immediately; I want you to have just what you want. You mean so much to me," he said. He's a dear. Our small storms just drift away.

Shirley, 50s ■

3. *Spiritual health is better than physical health.* I'm shaken every time I read Jesus' statements that if my hand or foot or eye causes me to sin, I should get rid of the hand or foot or eye because "it is better for you to enter life crippled than to have two feet and be thrown into hell" (Mark 9:45).

That goes against everything in me that says my physical health and comfort are my inalienable rights. Hearing Dr. Helen Roseveare speak helped me to get this in perspective. Dr. Roseveare is an English medical missionary doctor who worked in Zaire for many years. She suffered terribly at the hands of her captors during the civil war there.

After she returned to England, she discovered that she had breast cancer. After all that she had already suffered physically, it was unbelievable that such a thing should happen to her. As she struggled to reconcile her situation with what she knew about God's character, she clearly heard God saying to her: "Can you not trust me? I know what I am doing. This cancer is only in the body, after all, so what does it matter in the light of eternity?"

Afterward, in follow-up clinics, she began to realize what God's purpose may have been. As she sat in the silent waiting room of a cancer clinic with other women who, like herself, had all had breast surgery, she tried to share her peace of mind with the fearful woman next to her.

"Do you mind if I share with you why I am not afraid?" she asked quietly.

"Not at all," said the startled woman, through her tears. "Tell me!"

As she began, Dr. Roseveare soon realized that all the women in the waiting room were listening to her as she explained how God had freed her from her fears. Because of England's nationalized medical service, she was able to take her records with her and go to follow-up clinics in any town where she was visiting. So she has had the opportunity to share her testimony not only in churches and conferences all over the English-speaking world in recent years, but also all over England as she sat in a clinic waiting room.

4. *Obedience is better than sacrifice.* I'm sobered by Jesus' statement that obedience is the test of our love for him (see John 15:10-14). The chief commandment is to love God with all our being. Since love is a subjective feeling, we're never sure if we love "enough." But obedience is objective and specific.

Sometimes we're tempted to think that sacrifice is a better demonstration of our love than obedience. If we're so busy in church meetings, committees, and other Christian activities that we sacrifice time with our families or rest for ourselves,

God must be impressed. But when we compare that with God's priorities, we see our error.

5. *Faith is better than feelings and sight.* We like to see where we're going and how things are going to turn out. But as I discussed in the chapter on trust, God asks us to trust his character even in the dark.

A helpful illustration pictures *faith* as tightrope walker. He is walking a rope across Niagara Falls. Ahead of *faith* is the first walker, *facts*. Behind him comes the third walker, *feelings*. When *faith* turns around to look at *feelings,* he is in trouble.

Our faith needs to keep looking at the facts about God and what he has done. Our changing feelings don't stimulate faith, but as we act in faith, our feelings begin to catch up.

6. *Serving is better than being served.* What a radical thought! I like going to a motel where someone else makes the bed and cleans the bathroom. I like being served dinner while I sit comfortably enjoying the atmosphere and the food.

The value of serving was the theme of the commencement address at the University of Pennsylvania's Wharton School of Business in May 1985. Our son-in-law, Paul, was one of the graduates receiving advice from the former head of the General Electric Corporation. He told the M.B.A. graduates that to be leaders they would need followers.

He said the way to have followers is to serve people. Serve the people under you by praising their efforts and affirming their good work and their value. Serve the people above you by asking, What will benefit the company? What can I do to help my boss reach his goals?

The greatest way I can serve a person is to help her know God and grow in godliness. Serving involves encouraging a person to investigate who Jesus is, raising questions about her reason for living and what she believes about Jesus, being her friend, and praying for her.

It isn't either living a godly life before her or speaking about Jesus; it's both. As Paul Little asks in his book *How to Give Away Your Faith,* "Which wing of an airplane is more important, the right or the left?" No one can guess how to become a Christian by just watching a godly person.

Sometimes I remind myself of the four lepers who were starving when the city of Samaria was under siege. They decided to go out to the enemy camp to beg for food. If they got killed, they wouldn't be worse off than if they starved in the city. But when they got to the camp, they found it deserted. They feasted on what the army left. They took silver, gold, and clothes and hid them. When they returned for a third load, they realized what they were doing. They said, "We're not doing right. This is a day of good news and we are keeping it to ourselves" (2 Kings 7:9). If we keep the Good News about Jesus to ourselves, we are not fully serving people or obeying Jesus.

Most of our choices along the path to godliness are between the good and the better. Our awareness of sin and the Holy Spirit alert us to blatant evil. But the subtle temptation to substitute something good—such as beauty, security, health—for what God says is better slips up on us like a hungry lion on a wounded zebra. Testing society's competing values against God's values exposes them for what they are and enables us to choose the better.

Chapter Twenty-One

Walking in Step

Along the way, choosing responses

As I pulled my soggy sheets out of the washer one Wednesday morning, gray spots appeared all over them. It was a shocking apparition, because the sheets didn't go into the washer that way. Still more curious than angry, I inspected them closely. They were not random spots. Their pattern matched that of the holes in the washer drum. In dismay, I quickly grabbed one of Jim's white shirts. Gray spots littered the material as if it had been spatter painted. Obviously, the washer had betrayed me, so I stuffed the whole load of whites in again, punched the buttons to let the machine know who was boss, and orbited the clothes through another cycle. Voila! Everything came out clean and sparkling.

For weeks after that, I dreaded lifting the lid after a washer run. What would I behold? Clean white sheets, or sheets flecked with gray? More often than not, the hated spots assaulted me and tried to ruin my day. So I had to make a choice. I could let them turn me inside out and make me angry, grouchy, and filled with self-pity. Or I could relax and throw them back into the washer.

When I chose not to let the washer get the better of me, the potential disaster turned into positive advantage for me and my family. The right choice kept me from being victimized by my circumstances. God shows us how to grow in godliness even in such mundane things as doing the laundry.

One of my biggest challenges in writing this book was learning to use a word processor. Sure enough, one day it locked me out. The computer "ate" two hours' worth of my painstaking work. Totally helpless, I called the computer store and described my problem to Keith, the manager.

"I'm afraid I don't know what happened. I really don't know why you got locked out. But I do know you can't get it back," he said.

"This is a black day!" I exclaimed, still not fully accepting the awful truth.

Surprised by my reaction, he said, "I usually get more expletives than that when this happens."

His humor reduced the tension. Strangely, I could actually smile to myself. Thank God I didn't blast Keith. I don't possess perfect self-control, by any means, but I've made some progress since the time I irately accused Jim of selfishness and bad motives when he took Sara for a walk on Sunday morning.

Stories from the Journey

 Five years ago I married Franklin, age 68, and became stepmother to his children, who were all my age. Desperately wanting their immediate acceptance and approval, I worried about the implications of everything I said and they said. *What do they think of me? Why did she say that? Am I resented? Am I welcome? Was that remark a put-down?* When a friend told me acceptance would happen in time. I thought she meant, in time the family would change.

But guess who needed to change? My focus needed to move from getting love for myself to loving my husband and his children. Gradually I realized that my first responsibility is to love my husband, their father. If I want love, I first have to give it.

When a painful situation arises, I have learned to pour out my heart to God and my husband instead of stewing inside. With a quick prayer for help, I can return a soft answer or silence instead of a caustic remark.

During family visits conversations often arise about the past. At first I resented being left out. But pouting through an evening in boredom isn't any fun. Once I realized that these conversations supplied some missing pieces to this puzzle called Franklin Harris, I began to listen eagerly for the stories that fill in the gaps. Hearing the family experiences I missed helps me understand Franklin better—his personality, habits, joys, and sorrows.

Marrying a retiree brought me lots of opportunities to choose my responses. Overnight I shifted from full-time employment to unstructured days. My creative, scientific husband didn't have enough time in the day to do all he wanted to do. I, on the other hand, wondered what to do with my time. My overzealous attention to Franklin's activities paralyzed me. My jealousy over his passion for computers kept me from seeing his computer knowledge as a way to serve God and help others.

Instead of complaining about time on my hands, I needed to see it as an opportunity. Once I began to pray about how to use the marvelous gift of time, happy possibilities abounded. God even made a dream come true. In 1992 Franklin and I spent three months in Ecuador using our talents as missionary volunteers.

Karen, 40s ■

What's the basic issue in all of this? Godliness is intensely practical, but we can't manufacture it. It grows with training in making the right choices.

For example, I prefer peace, joy, kindness, gentleness, patience, and self-control to violence, rage, envy, and hatred. That's another way of saying that I prefer the fruit that the Holy Spirit produces in me rather than the consequences of wrong choices. My run-ins with the washing machine and the computer were just part of God's on-the-job training for me. I had to choose to let the Holy Spirit do in me what I could not do for myself.

Godly qualities are called the fruit of the Holy Spirit. Fruit isn't something we can create. We can't manufacture an

8

apple. When an apple tree's limbs bow under the weight of luscious fruit, we know it's a genuine apple tree, fulfilling the purpose of its creation. Only the Holy Spirit can produce the luscious fruit of

- love, joy, peace,
- patience, kindness, goodness,
- faithfulness, gentleness, self-control.

Think of Jesus. Picture what he was like. Didn't all of these godly traits characterize his life? Here is the stunning secret. As the Holy Spirit produces fruit in us, he makes us more like Jesus, which has been God's plan from the beginning.

Stories from the Journey

 Last year ended with some serious problems, and the new year brought a fresh supply. I'm having trouble dealing with it all and not feeling very far down the path to godliness. But it helps to remember that being a godly woman is the desire of my heart and certainly what God wants for me. Some days I'm impatient with the process. Other days I know that as long as I'm going forward I'm making progress.

Linda, 40s, mother of three ■

To grasp how the Spirit does for us what we can't do, picture a boxing ring. Two fighters slug it out—the Holy

Spirit in me and the evil desires of my human nature. I'm the referee. By my choice, I decide who wins each round. The Spirit is far superior to my sinful ways, yet I have to let him win, so to speak.

We make the right choice when we decide the Spirit will win. That's what happened on that Thanksgiving Day when I chose to worship God after he had said no to my prayer for a baby. I make a wrong choice when I allow some kind of sin to win. My exploding at the pharmacist illustrates that choice. God gives me the total power of the Holy Spirit, but I must make the right choices. It's either the life-giving, fruit-producing Spirit, or the defeat and despair of my selfishness and pride.

God holds us accountable for our choices. No one else will answer for you. We can't blame anyone or anything for our choices. People and circumstances influence us, but every day we choose.

On the other hand, God does for us what we can't do for ourselves. He does what no one else can do for us. He gives us life, forgiveness, mercy, worth, identity, completeness. But best of all, on the path to godliness God is conforming us to the image of the Lord Jesus. We have the freedom to choose to walk in step with the Spirit or to stubbornly dig in our heels. You can choose the most significant transformation in your life—a life of godliness, of being Christlike in a world that sees so very little of him.

We can walk the path with confidence and joy because "his divine power has given us *everything we need for life and godliness* through our knowledge of him who called us by his own glory and goodness" (2 Peter 1:3, italics added).

Chapter Twenty-Two

We Finally Made It

Along the way, your heart's desire

When I first discovered "Delight yourself in the Lord and he will give you the desires of your heart" (Psalm 37:4), I thought it meant that if I served God, he'd give me whatever I wanted. But as I knew God better, I realized that he changes my desires. He gives me new desires that he knows will satisfy my deepest longings.

In this chapter I want to tell you about two of those heart's desires that God has given me. The first is the closeness Sara and I enjoy today. In chapter four, I told you of my first prayers for Sara that sprang from: "We love because he (God) first loved us" (1 John 4:19). "Lord, help me to so love Sara that she will feel loved and be completely convinced that I really do love her."

As we adjusted to being a family, I often remembered the advice my sister, Jerry, gave me. "If you have struggles with Sara and John, don't necessarily blame it on being a stepmother. I've worked with lots of parents who struggle with their birth children for different reasons."

I soon knew that Sara and I approached life differently. When we shopped for an Easter hat, the third one she tried on looked darling. I was ready to leave. But five-year-old Sara had to try on every hat in the store before choosing that one.

Our differences showed up in decorating Easter eggs. My goal was to get the eggs cooked, colored, and in the baskets as quickly as possible. Sara's goal was to create a work of art on each egg. With a small brush, she patiently painted delicate flowers, trees, butterflies, or a rainbow on the colored eggs. If I stayed in the kitchen, my impatience with this long, tedious process spoiled the atmosphere. So I decided I should go for a walk, leaving Sara to enjoy painting in peace. Years later when we could talk about our differences, I asked Sara what would have helped her more. "I wish you had just sat and talked with me while I painted."

How obvious that sounds now. My leaving conveyed disapproval, not my desire to give her space to do her thing. Because we didn't talk enough about our feelings, we kept misinterpreting each other's actions and ascribing wrong motives. We wasted years and energy trying to please each other and never feeling we succeeded.

I became aware of Sara's second-guessing her choices and uncertainty about who she is as an adult. Our failure to feel really accepted and comfortable with one another must be part of the problem, I was sure. But miles apart emotionally and geographically, how do we start to open the painful subject? By taking a risk.

I remember the day I called to tell her that I heard her pain and wept with her. I wasn't calling to criticize but to be her encourager. I determined to *listen*. And the more I listened, the freer Sara talked. How I regretted the times I had answered instead of listening. With each phone call and visit, we cautiously examined past hurts and explained why we behaved as we did and the motives behind our words or actions. Our comfort zone expanded like the Texas sky. We could ask about events and feelings we had never discussed before.

In May 1991, Jim and I drove to Dallas to deliver some chairs to Paul and Sara. While the fellows played golf, Sara and I basked in the joy of each other's company while we cooked, explored the art museum, and sipped cappuccino under a live oak tree. No need to fight to be accepted any more.

As we said our good-byes on Monday, Sara's hug and kiss spoke volumes. Another *Memorial Day* to remember.

"I'm sorry it took so long for you to really know that I love you," I whispered to Sara as we hugged.

"But we finally made it!" she replied.

With tears of joy we celebrated the end of twenty-nine years of trying to please each other and never succeeding. We finally received the desire of our hearts, for mother and daughter to be comfortable in each other's love.

The next December Exxon moved Sara and Paul to Santiago, Chile. But Sara's invitation for me to come in May for the birth of their first baby made the distance bearable. Cathcrinc Leigh Schmidt arrived at 10:19 P.M., May 7, 1992, with auburn curls, blue eyes, and long fingers. Gathered around Sara's bed we praised God for a safe delivery and a healthy baby. We delighted in God and our latest fulfilled desire.

The second heart's desire God has granted came from a request I made after John's death. I asked God for other "sons," young men and women to love, mother, influence. In the church, several special relationships developed. I listened to their dreams and struggles. I prayed for them and for John's friends to respond to what God wanted to do in their lives. We shared hugs and encouragement freely. Some kept in touch when we moved to Illinois. I thanked God for every evidence that he was allowing us to have a part in the lives of these sons.

But God had a more specific answer to the desire of my heart. In the fall of 1986, Jim and I began to plan for his six months sabbatical. We needed someone to live in our house while we taught at Columbia Graduate School and Seminary in South Carolina and visited the Middle East. Where could we find a young man who'd like to live in our guest room, learn the peculiarities of our house and yard, and have the skills to maintain them while we were away?

Jim asked a friend if he knew anyone looking for a place to live. Yes, as a matter of fact, a young man had just joined the staff of a missions magazine in the same building where Jim had his office. So a few nights later, Scott came to visit. He had lived in many parts of the country, been on his own several years, just graduated from Moody Bible Institute, enjoyed writing, felt apprehensive about his first editorial job, needed a place to live, knew how to do simple repairs, and loved shoveling snow since he grew up in Syracuse.

As we toured the house and explained our needs and expectations, we felt drawn to this soft-spoken, thoughtful young man. A few days later, Scott dropped into Jim's office to say he'd like to move in. We were delighted. I adjusted the amount I cooked for supper. The premeasured four-ounce portions I'd been serving Jim and myself looked lonely on Scott's plate.

One day Scott asked about the pictures of John in a large frame and the stuffed duck on the family room wall. I explained the canoe trip on which John took most of the pictures and that the duck was John's first trophy.

"I'm surprised that you keep pictures and remembrances of John on display and talk about him so freely. My mother died when I was eleven. All her pictures and anything that belonged to her disappeared. It was like she never existed," Scott confided.

Sharing that painful memory started us on the journey to becoming a family. We talked about grief, how long it lasts, the importance of facing the pain and working through it, how unresolved grief erupts in our lives in unexpected ways. We shared our spiritual journeys. Scott quizzed Jim, a veteran editor, about how to live with deadlines. Over popcorn, Scott's favorite snack, we exchanged memories of places we loved: Colorado, Washington, mountains, the north woods, the ocean.

As Scott grew increasingly comfortable with us and with his job, he decided he was ready to deal with his past pain. Through months of working with a wise counselor, he gained insight and confidence in God and in himself. We listened and prayed. "Having a safe, peaceful place to live enabled me to face counseling," he told us later.

One day I realized it was time to tell Scott about my prayer in 1977. "When John died, I asked God for other sons. I believe you are an answer to that prayer," I confided to him. In God's gracious plan, he had brought another motherless son into my home and heart.

In the next two years, we shared the ups and downs of his romance with Carol Joy. When he finally decided to propose, he created his own videotape, played on our VCR. What fun to hear Carol Joy's description of her surprise and Scott's apprehension as he waited for the tape to reach the crucial moment. Birthday parties, dinners, a bridal shower filled our house with laughter and happy memories. After their engagement, their church planned a service of blessing during the morning worship. Scott honored Jim and me with the privilege of giving a personal blessing to him and Carol Joy. The week before their wedding, Jim and I directed a camp in Upper Michigan. A 4:00 A.M. departure got us to the church in time to bask in the joy of this son and daughter God had brought into our lives.

Cards for birthdays, Mother's Day and Father's Day, and Christmas visits continue to nourish our love and sense of family. I cherish Scott's Mother's Day cards, especially his notes. "You helped me understand the wondrous joy of being adopted into God's family by allowing me to be part of your family. Thanks for being a loving 'Mom' to this adopted son."

Delight yourself in the Lord, and He will give you the desires of your heart.

Psalm 37:4

Appendix

Help for Survivors of Childhood Sexual Abuse

The healing process requires specific tools:

1. A professional counselor, equipped to help survivors walk through their memories.
2. A journal for their insights and feelings.
3. A network of friends who listen and care. Peers who treat them as equals.
4. For some, a support group of other survivors that helps them walk through their grief.
5. Time. Lots of time.

My friends have taught me the following do's and don'ts about how a friend can help a survivor of abuse.

Do
1. Listen to her pain. Assure her she is not alone.
2. Affirm that God is involved in the healing. She and God are partners in the process.

3. Recognize her losses and grieve with her.

4. Remember, grief is a *slow* process.

5. Believe her. As memories emerge or events trigger unexplainable responses, she wavers between facing the truth or going back into denial.

6. Believe in her. Tell her how you see God in her life.

7. Affirm her getting professional help. If you are part of her primary support system, you may have questions that you need to ask the counselor rather than your friend. Written permission can be given for you to talk with the counselor. Counselors have clarified issues for me so I better understand my friends and the healing process.

8. Affirm that God knows and feels her pain, loves and accepts her, and wants her healing.

9. Affirm that depression ends. This pain will pass.

10. Pray for her healing, especially when she can't pray for herself. Ask God to comfort and instruct her through the Bible and other reading.

11. Trust God for her healing. One friend holds on to God's promise to her that the house she moved into will be a "house of healing." On an especially black day she called. "I need to hear someone say God is involved in this unbearable pain." Over the phone, I could remind her of God's promise to her and pray for her.

12. Keep confidences.

13. Be a knowledgeable support. Read to understand the process.

Don't
1. Shun her.
2. Be judgmental of her anger and struggles.
3. Play God in her life by telling her what to do. God is the healer, not you.
4. Use the Bible as a Band-Aid for her deep wounds.
5. Talk about forgiveness before she has grieved her losses.
6. Say, "That's all over. Just forget and forgive."

What can a church do to help?
1. Emphasize the need to integrate spiritual and emotional healing.
2. Give emotional and physical support during the healing process. Help pay for counseling if necessary.
3. Find a qualified professional who can supervise and advise a support group for survivors.
4. Grieve with the survivor.

Suggested Reading
Child Sexual Abuse: A Hope for Healing by Maxine Hancock and Karen Mains

A Door of Hope by Jan Frank

Surviving the Secret Healing: The Hurt of Sexual Abuse by Paula Vredevelt and K. Rodignez

We Weep for Ourselves and Our Children: A Christian Guide for Survivors of Childhood Sexual Abuse by Joanne Feldmeth and Midge Finley